CW00456706

Tourism Planning
and
Tour Operation

Tourism Planning and Tour Operation

Dr. Devesh Nigam
Assistant Professor
Institute of Tourism & Hotel Management
Bundelkhand University
Jhansi (U.P.)

SHREE PUBLISHERS & DISTRIBUTORS
NEW DELHI-110 002

Edition : 2008

Published by :
SHREE PUBLISHERS & DISTRIBUTORS
4735/22, Prakash Deep Building
Ansari Road, Darya Ganj,
New Delhi–110 002

ISBN : 978-81–8329–276–4

Printed by :
Adi Shree Printers
Delhi–110 091

PREFACE

Tourism planning and tour operation comprehensively discusses various aspects of the business of tourism in the Indian context. Delineating systematically the functions of the tour operation in tourism, the book provides a set of tools for managing tourism problems, monitoring policy and its implementation, promoting sites etc. It analyses the dynamics of formulating appropriate tourism policy.

Blending current trends in the travel and tourism field with the emerging range of opportunities and challenges the book gives a valuable insight into the intricacies of the works and problems related to tourism. With an all-encompassing, sharp reading into the tourism field, the book would be an invaluable read for tour operators, guides and anybody in the travel and tourism arena.

Devesh Nigam

CONTENTS

CHAPTER 1

TOURISM PLANNING

A tourist is usually defined as a person who travels for non-business reasons more than 50 miles from and overnights away from her usual place of residence. It is around this definition, or ones like it, that most travel statistics-departures, expenditures-are compiled and computed. From among a multitude of other definitions of tourism, there are two important views on what tourism is that have ramifications for successful tourism planning. First, there is the view that tourism is an individual human experience which some anthropologists theorize is really ritual human cultural experience. The second view is that tourism is an export economic activity. Individual experiences of the tourist are key to the success of any tourism strategy. It is often that dream of a future experience at some place other than at home or at the office which motivates people to travel and become tourists. It is the guaranteed repeat of pleasant experiences that brings a tourist back a second time or inspires one to "spread the word" about this wonderful destination to others. A successful tourism strategy must therefore, provided desired experiences or people will not come the first time or will not come back for a second.

There is one anthropological theory which proposes that tourism is ritual experience akin to religious experience. Because a tourism experience is limited in time for most people, and it occurs for them in an out-of-the-ordinary place, there can be feelings of extraordinary reality associated with a destination. When one takes a trip, one leaves one's ordinary life through a transition, like an airplane flight; one has heightened liminal, some would say spiritual, experiences at this extraordinary, mystical place, and then one returns to ordinary life through another transition, a coming down. Grieving the loss of the mystical place and the intense relationships that were experienced there frequently accompany this last transition. When people are in the time and space of their extraordinary, mystical place, the rules of their ordinary lives are usually suspended or may be totally reversed. They are susceptible to seeing fate in chance occurrences, they experience déja vu, they use only first names, they get drunk in public, and they have amorous, sometimes sexual, encounters with strangers whom they will never see again.

Tourism can also be viewed as a special case of export economic activity. It is a special case because rather than shipping goods and service products out to the purchaser, the purchaser comes to the point of origin of the goods and services in order to procure-experience-them. This is the phenomena that can lead to the many undesirable externalities-congestion, pollution, crime-that occur in tourism development. This is the root of the tourism paradox and what brings ruin to the goose that lays the golden eggs of tourism's economic benefit.

Several tourism classification systems have been devised to help describe tourists and modes of tourism consistently. One nominal classification focuses on the primary type of attraction(s) that is being emphasized in the tourism product which is being marketed and delivered. Examples include:

— Ecotourism
— Nature tourism

— Adventure tourism

— Getaway and stay

— Cultural tourism

Another is an ordinal classification that is based on tourist party volumes. This measure ranges from mass tourism for large numbers of tourists to explorer for the single tourist traveling by herself.

Planning of tourism includes drawing up the future that can be acceptable to the local inhabitants and visitors. Without planning and controlling mechanism the development of tourism may end by having social, cultural and economic distortions, which will be reflected in the relationship between tourists and local inhabitants.

As soon as the tourism grows and expands, it brings the social and economical changes in the respective region. These can be positive as well as negative. There are choices to deal with them:

1. To react on the changes after they happens ;

2. To forecast them and to develop method or plan to be able prevent and control in the best way.

The second is more advanced as it is based on planning. The efficiency of tourism can be shown with:

1. Positive economical impacts:

    — tourism helps to diversify and stabilize economic of region;

    — makes good basis for current business and provide circumstances for new businesses;

    — demand for additional employees;

    — increase of turnover creates increase of incomes;

    — the turnover and additional incomes make increase of taxes in the budget.

2.   Positive social impacts:

— the pride of native place from local inhabitants increases;.

— new social contacts appear;

— revenues from tourism help to support the cultural and historical objects;

— increases educational level of the inhabitants;

— tourism helps develop the trade and don't allow to disappear the particular culture and customs ;

— development of the culture and crafts promotes.

3.   Positive environmental impacts:

— saves flora and fauna ;

— maintain of the natural objects;

— care taking of the environment.

Inadequately planned and developed tourism can cause the problems.

1.   Negative social aspects are:

— congestion;

— life style conflicts;

— criminal level;

— tension with the local inhabitants for the use of the tourism resources.

2.   The negative factors influencing environment are:

— increase of the wastage;

— increase of pollution, noise ;

— the rear species could diminish;

— there could be the damages of the physical environment.

For prevention of negative aspects, careful tourism resources analyse and planning of the future actions, oriented on the sustainable tourism should be made. During the planning process Latvia tries to avoid the negative factors and increases the positive influence of the social, economical, and environmental factors, which are connected with tourism development. The tourism planners must to be sure, that tourism will give maximum positive impact for the municipality. The planning process is associated with the following points:

1. Developing of high-level tourism sector must not always be very expensive.

2. To encourage use the tourism either for cultural and economical exchange.

3. Distribute the economical gains from the tourism to the possible more local people.

4. To preserve the cultural and natural resources as the part of the tourism development..

5. To maximise the income of the foreign tourists for the stabilization of the payment balance.

6. To increase employment.

7. To help the peripheral regions increase the employment and prevent the outflow of the local people.

8. To increase the number of the "high income class" tourists.

Currently, the economical objectives are dominating in Latvia, however we should not forget others, especially, if want to develop long-term plan. After analysing several tourism development plans, and by taking into account the current situation, conclusions could be made that in the basis tourism plans divides in the three planning stages:

1. research and analyses;

2. conformity of the current and planned tourism activities to the social, economical and environmental goals;

3. the development system control.

Those three stages includes following tourism development planning steps:

1. The goal setting.
2. The evaluation of the current situation.
3. Setting the tourism policy and priorities.
4. The formulation of the strategy
5. The evaluation of the impacts.
6. The implementation of the policy and the projects.
7. The control and contingency.

The analysing of tourism plans and development strategy shows, that the tourism industry consists of three important and interdependent sectors:

— Business sector or entrepreneurs;

— Non - governmental organisations;

— Government (national, regional, local level).

The private and public sector has the different view on the tourism development. The entrepreneurs are focusing on the profitable projects. At the same time, the public sector has different criteria: to create working places, to increase tax income, to improve the infrastructure.The government contributes in the tourism development for the political reasons, for example, the improving situation in some regions may impact the development of whole country. The government has the main role in regulation and supervision of industry by taking in force the respective legislation. Although government can participate in the planning process and often government or state is the owner of the tourism facilities or the land.

PROCESS OF TOURISM PLANNING

Tourism planning has evolved from two related but distinct sets of planning philosophies and methods. On the one hand, tourism is one of many activities in an area that must be considered as part of physical, environmental, social, and economic planning. Therefore, it is common to find tourism addressed, at least partially, in a regional land use, transportation, recreation, economic development, or comprehensive plan.

The degree to which tourism is addressed in such plans depends upon the relative importance of tourism to the community or region and how sensitive the planning authority is to tourism activities. Tourism may also be viewed as a business in which a community or region chooses to engage. Individual tourism businesses conduct a variety of planning activities including feasibility, marketing, product development, promotion, forecasting, and strategic planning. If tourism is a significant component of an area's economy or development plans, regional or community-wide marketing plans are needed to coordinate the development and marketing activities of different tourism interests in the community.

A comprehensive approach integrates a strategic marketing plan with more traditional public planning activities. This ensures a balance between serving the needs and wants of the tourists versus the needs and wants of local residents. A formal tourism plan provides a vehicle for the various interests within a community to coordinate their activities and work toward common goals. It also is a means of coordinating tourism with other community activities.

Like any planning, tourism planning is goal-oriented, striving to achieve certain objectives by matching available resources and programs with the needs and wants of people. Comprehensive planning requires a systematic approach, usually involving a series of steps.

The process is best viewed as an iterative and on-going one, with each step subject to modification and refinement at any stage of the planning process. There are six steps in the planning process:

— Define goals and objectives.
— Identify the tourism system.
    — Resources
    — Organizations
    — Markets
— Generate alternatives.
— Evaluate alternatives.
— Select and implement.
— Monitor and evaluate.

Setting Goals and Objectives

Obtaining clear statements of goals and objectives is difficult, but important. Ideally, tourism development goals should flow from more general community goals and objectives. It is important to understand how a tourism plan serves these broader purposes. If tourism is identified as a means of serving broader community goals, it makes sense to develop plans with more specific tourism development objectives. These are generally defined through a continuing process in which various groups and organizations in a community work together toward common goals.

A local planning authority, chamber of commerce, visitors bureau, or similar group should assume a leadership role to develop an initial plan and obtain broad involvement of tourism interests in the community. Public support for the planning process and plan is also important. Having a good understanding of tourism and the tourism system in your community is the first step toward defining goals and objectives for tourism development.

The types of goals that are appropriate and the precision with which you are able to define them will depend upon how long your community has been involved in tourism and tourism planning. In the early stages of tourism development, goals may involve establishing organizational structures and collecting information to better identify the tourism system in the community. Later, more precise objectives can be formulated and more specific development and marketing strategies evaluated.

Defining the Tourism System

When planning for any type of activity, it is important to first define its scope and characteristics. Tourism is defined in many ways. Generally, tourism involves people traveling outside of their community for pleasure. Definitions differ on the specifics of how far people must travel, whether or not they must stay overnight, for how long, and what exactly is included under traveling for "pleasure". Do you want your tourism plan to include day visitors, conventioneers, business travelers, people visiting friends and relatives, people passing through, or seasonal residents? Which community resources and organizations serve tourists or could serve tourists? Generally, tourists share community resources with local residents and businesses.

Many organizations serve both tourists and locals. This complicates tourism planning and argues for a clear idea of what your tourism plan entails. You can begin to clarify the tourism system by breaking it down into three subsystems:

— tourism resources,

— tourism organizations, and

— tourism markets.

An initial task in developing a tourism plan is to identify, inventory, and classify the objects within each of these subsystems.

Tourism resources

Tourism resources are any (1) natural, (2) cultural, (3) human, or (4) capital resources that either are used or can be used to attract or serve tourists. A tourism resource inventory identifies and classifies the resources available that provide opportunities for tourism development. Conduct an objective and realistic assessment of the quality and quantity of resources you have to work with. Important Tourism Resources are the following:

— Natural Resources

    — Climate-seasons

    — Water resources-lakes, streams, waterfalls

    — Flora-forests, flowers, shrubs, wild edibles

    — Fauna-fish & wildlife

    — Geological resources-topography, soils, sand dunes, beaches, caves, rocks & minerals, fossils

    — Scenery-combinations of all of the above

— Cultural Resources

    — Historic buildings, sites

    — Monuments, shrines

    — Cuisine

    — Ethnic cultures

    — Industry, government, religion, etc.

    — Anthropological resources

    — Local celebrities

- Human Resources
  - Hospitality skills
  - Management skills
  - Seasonal labor force
  - Performing artists-music, drama, art, storytellers, etc.
  - Craftsman and artisans
  - Other labor skills from chefs to lawyers to researchers
  - Local populations
- Capital
  - Availability of capital, financing
  - Infrastructure-transportation roads, airports, railroads, harbors & marinas, trails & walkways
  - Infrastructure: utilities water, power, waste treatment, communications

Tourism organization

Tourism organization combine resources in various proportions to provide products and services for the tourist. It is important to recognize the diverse array of public and private organizations involved with tourism. The most difficult part of tourism planning is to get these groups to work toward common goals. Setting up appropriate communication systems and institutional arrangements is a key part of community tourism planning.

Tourism management organisation and services

- *Coordination, planning, technical assistance, research, regulation:*
  - Federal & state departments of commerce, transportation, & natural resources

- — Federal, state, regional, & local tourism associations
- — Educational organizations & consultants, e.g., Travel & Tourism Research Association; U.S.
- — Travel information & reservation services
- — *Development, promotion and management, of tourism resources:*
  - — Federal agencies, NB. departments of commerce, transportation, & land management agencies
  - — State agencies, NB. departments of commerce, transportation, & land/facility management agencies
  - — Local government organizations, e.g., visitor information, chamber of commerce, convention & visitor's bureaus, parks
- — *Businesses:*
  - — Accommodations: Hotels, motels, Lodges, resorts, bed & breakfast cabins & cottages, Condominiums, second homes, Campgrounds
  - — Food & Beverage: Restaurants, Grocery, Bars, nightclubs,
- — *Fast food, Catering services:*
  - — *Transportation*: Air, rail, bus; Local transportation: taxi, limo, Auto, bicycle, boat rental; Local tour services
  - — Information: Travel agencies, Information and reservation services, Automobile clubs
- — *Recreation Facilities and Services*: Winter sports: ski, skating, snowmobile areas; Golf courses, miniature golf; Swimming pools, water slides, beaches; tennis, handball, racquetball courts, bowling alleys; Athletic clubs, health spas; Marinas, boat rentals and charters; hunting & fishing guides; Horseback enterprises; Sporting goods sales & rentals

— *Entertainment*: Nightclubs, amusement parks, spectator sport facilities; Gambling facilities: casinos, horse racing, bingo; video arcades; art galleries and studios, craft shops, studios, demonstrations; performing arts: theater, dance, music, film; historic & prehistoric sites; museums: art, history, science, technology; arboreta, zoos, nature centers,

— Special festivals and events.

— *Support services*: Auto repair, gasoline service stations; boat & recreation vehicle dealers and service; retail shops: sporting goods, specialties, souvenirs, clothing; health services: hospitals, clinics, pharmacies; laundry and dry cleaning; beauty & barber shops; babysitting services; pet care; communications: newspaper, telephone; banking and financial services

Tourism markets

Tourists makeup the third, and perhaps most important subsystem. Successful tourism programs require a strong market orientation. The needs and wants of the tourists you choose to attract and serve must be the focus of much of your marketing and development activity. Therefore, it is important to clearly understand which tourism market segments you wish to attract and serve. Tourists fall into a very diverse set of categories with quite distinct needs and wants. A visitor survey identifies the size and nature of the existing market and asks the following questions:

— What are the primary market segments you presently attract?

— Where do they come from?

— What local businesses and facilities do they use?

— What attracted them to the community?

— How did they find out about your community?

— How satisfied are they with your offerings?

A market survey (usually a telephone survey) also can be conducted among households in regions from which you wish to attract tourists. This type of study helps identify potential markets, and means of attracting tourists to your area.

Tourism market segments: In a general tourism plan, some clear target tourism market segments should be identified. You might begin by defining the market area from which you will draw most of your visitors. The size of your market area depends upon the uniqueness and quality of your "product", transportation systems, tastes and preferences of surrounding populations, and your competition.

Identifying the market area will help target information and promotion and define transportation routes and modes, competition, and characteristics of the market. Next, divide the travel market into the following trip length categories:

— day trips from a 50 mile radius,

— day trips from 50 to 200 miles away,

— pass-through travelers,

— overnight trips of 1 or 2 nights (most likely weekends), and

— extended overnight vacation trips.

After have an idea of your market area and kinds of trips you will be serving, begin defining more specific market segments like vehicle campers, downhill skiers, sightseers, family vacationers, single weekenders, and the like. These segments can be more clearly tied to particular resources, businesses, and facilities in your community. Tourism market segments are given the following:

I. Geographic market areas
II. Trip categories
— Day Trips:
   — short-within 50 miles
   — long-up to 200 miles
— Pass through traffic:
   — day visitors
   — overnight stays
— Overnight Trips:
   — weekend
   — vacation
III. Activity or trip purpose
— Outdoor Recreation:
   — Water-based Activity:
   — Boating: sail, power, cruise, row, canoe, water ski
   — Swimming: pool, beach, sunbathing, scuba
   — Fishing: charter, sport, from pier, boat, shore, ice
   — Land-based Activity:
   — Camping: backpacking, primitive, developed
   — Hiking: climbing, beachcombing, spelunking
   — Hunting
   — Skiing: downhill, cross country
   — Snowmobiling
   — Bicycling
   — Horseback riding
   — Picnicking
   — Air-based Activity:
   — Airplane rides, hang gliding, ballooning, parachuting

— General:
  — Nature study
  — Photography or landscape painting
  — Viewing natural scenery
— Sightseeing & Entertainment:
  — Visiting particular sites or areas:
  — historic or pre-historic
  — cultural
  — amusements
  — scenic
  — Attending particular events, shows, o demonstrations:
  — ethnic festivals
  — sporting events
  — performances
  — agricultural fair or festival
  — boat show
  — shopping
— Other Primary Purpose for Trip:
  — Visiting Friends & Relatives
  — Convention & Business/Pleasure

Tourist needs as well as their impact on the local community are quite different for day tourists versus overnight tourists. Areas catering primarily to weekend traffic will experience large fluctuations in use. In deciding the relative importance of these different segments, communities need to assess both their ability to provide required services, as well as the demand for different types of trips relative to the supply and your competition.

Environment: A tourism plan is significantly affected by many factors in the broader environment. Indeed, one of the complexities of tourism planning is the number of variables that are outside of the control of an individual tourism business or community. These include such things as tourism offerings and prices at competing destinations, federal and state policy and legislation, currency exchange rates, the state of the economy, and weather.

Local populations also must be considered in tourism planning. As they compete with tourists for resources, they can be significantly affected by tourism activity, and they are an important source of support in getting tourism plans implemented. A survey of local residents can be conducted to assess community attitudes toward tourism development, identify impacts of tourism on the community, and obtain local input into tourism plans. Public hearings, workshops, and advisory boards are other ways to obtain public involvement in tourism planning. Local support and cooperation is important to the success of tourism programs and should not be overlooked.

Generating Alternative Development Options

Generating alternative development and marketing options to meet your goals requires some creative thinking and brainstorming. The errors made at this stage are usually thinking too narrowly or screening out alternatives prematurely. It is wise to solicit a wide range of options from a diverse group of people. If tourism expertise is lacking in your community, seek help and advice outside the community. Tourism planning involves a wide range of interrelated development and marketing decisions. The following development questions will get you started:

— How much importance should be assigned to tourism within a community or region?

— Which general community goals is tourism development designed to serve?

— Which organization(s) will provide the leadership and coordination necessary for community tourism planning? What are the relative roles of public and private sectors?

Tourism marketing decision questions include:

— Segments: Which market segments should be pursued; geographic markets, trip types, activity or demographic subgroups?

— Product: What kinds of tourism products and services should be provided? Who should provide what?

— Place: Where should tourism facilities be located?

— Promotion: What kinds of promotion should be used, by whom, in which media, how much, when? What community tourism theme or image should be established?

— Price: What prices should be charged for which products and services. Who should capture the revenue?

Evaluating Alternative Options

Tourism development and marketing options are evaluated by assessing the degree to which each option will be able to meet the stated goals and objectives. There are usually two parts to a systematic evaluation of tourism development and marketing alternatives:

(1) Feasibility analysis, and

(2) Impact assessment.

These two tasks are interrelated, but think of them as trying to answer two basic questions: (1) Can it be done?, and (2) What are the consequences? A decision to take a specific action must be based both on feasibility and desirability.

Feasibility Analysis: First, screen alternatives and eliminate those that are not feasible due to economic, environmental, political, legal, or other factors. Evaluate the remaining set of alternatives in more detail, paying particular attention to the market potential and financial plan. Make a realistic assessment of your community's ability to attract and serve a market segment or segments.

This requires a clear understanding of the tourism market in your area and how this market is changing. Also carefully identify your competition and evaluate your advantages and disadvantages compared to the competition. Plan toward the future because it takes time to implement decisions and for your actions to take effect. Therefore, look at the likely market and competition for several years to come. Review forecasts for the travel market in your area, if available. Careful tracking of tourism trends in your own community can help identify changes in the market that you will have to adapt to.

When evaluating alternative development and marketing strategies it is important to understand the impacts, both positive and negative, of proposed actions. The types of impacts and their importance vary across different communities and proposed actions. Generally, the size, extent, and nature of tourism impacts depend upon:

— volume of tourist activity relative to local activity

— length and nature of tourist contacts with the community

— degree of concentration/dispersal of tourist activity in the area

— similarities or differences between local populations and tourists

— stability/sensitivity of local economy, environment, and social structure

— how well tourism is planned, controlled, and managed.

Look at both the benefits and costs of any proposed actions. While tourism development can increase income, revenues, and employment, it also involves costs. Evaluate benefits and costs of tourism development from the perspectives of local government, businesses, and residents.

Economic Impacts:

— Sales, revenue, and income

— Employment

— Fiscal impact-taxes, infrastructure costs

— Prices

— Economic base & structure

Environmental Impacts:

— Lands

— Waters

— Air

— Infrastructure

— Flora & fauna

Social Impacts:

— Population structure & distribution

— Values & attitudes

— Education

— Occupations

— Safety & security

— Congestion & crowding

— Community spirit & cohesion

— Quality of life

Impacts on Local Government: Local government provides most of the infrastructure and many of the services essential to tourism development, including highways, public parks, law enforcement, water and sewer, garbage collection and disposal.

Evaluate tourism decisions with a clear understanding of the capacity of the local infrastructure and services relative to anticipated needs, and take into account both the needs of local populations and tourists. A fiscal impact analysis evaluates the impact of tourism on the community's tax base and local government costs. It entails predicting the additional infrastructure and service requirements of tourism development, estimating their costs, deciding who will pay for/provide them, and how.

Impacts on Business and Industry: Businesses that are directly serving tourists benefit from sales to tourists. Through secondary impacts, tourism activity also benefits a wide range of businesses in a community. For example, a local textile industry may sell to a linen supply firm that serves hotels and motels catering primarily to tourists.

A local forest products industry sells to a lumberyard where local woodcarvers or furniture makers buy their supplies. They in turn sell to tourists through various retail outlets. All of these businesses benefit from tourism. If most products and services for tourists are bought outside of the local area, much of the tourist spending "leaks" out of the local economy. The more a community is "self-sufficient" in serving tourists, the larger the local impact.

Impacts on Residents: Local residents may experience a broad range of both positive and negative impacts from tourism development. Tourism development may provide increased employment and income for the community.

Although tourism jobs are primarily in the service sectors and are often seasonal, part time, and low-paying, these characteristics, are neither universal nor always undesirable. Residents may value opportunities for part time and seasonal work.

In particular, employment opportunities and work experiences for students or retirees may be desired. Residents may also benefit from local services that otherwise would not be available. Tourism development may mean a wider variety of retailers and restaurants, or a better community library. It may also mean more traffic, higher prices, and increases in property values and local taxes. The general quality of the environment and life in the community may go up or down due to tourism development. This depends on the nature of tourism development, the preferences and desires of local residents, and how well tourism is planned and managed.

A set of specific actions should be prescribed with clearly defined responsibilities and timetables. Monitor progress in implementing the plan and evaluate the success of the plan in meeting its goals and objectives on a regular basis. Plans generally need to be adjusted over time due to changing goals, changing market conditions, and unanticipated impacts. It is a good idea to build monitoring and evaluation systems into your planning efforts.

Structural COmponents of Tourism Plans

Structure of tourism in terms of the economic concepts of demand and supply. The importance of his analysis of tourism structure is that it points out that successful tourism depends on planning in two economic arenas, not just the one. There must be balance in creating both demand and supply or projects and plans will fail.

Demand

Demand in Gunn's model is population. The first cut of population into a tourist market occurs with the availability of two discretionary resources-time and money; this cut probably produces a potential global tourist market of certainly less than 10 percent of world's population. Refinement of the potential tourist population into specific market segments toward whom marketing campaigns and promotions are geared is a cash cow for many marketing and advertising consultants. The work involves survey research and sophisticated multi-variate statistical analysis of the results.

Supply

Gunn viewed supply as composed of four components: transportation, attractions, services and information and promotion. Transportation has to be considered on two levels. First is the linkage between the tourists' place of origin and their destination; the second is the destination region's transportation network. A complete planning process should consider provision of all aspects of physical infrastructure: transportation, water, sewer, energy and communications in this structural component. Attractions, and Gunn's attractions component should be explicitly expanded to include events, function in two ways in successful tourism planning. One is they are the magnets that often entice a person to travel to a particular destination, that dreamed experience, and second they are part of the real tourism experience of a destination region.

Service is the other significant experience generating component of tourism. The focus of this component is accommodation, and food and beverage establishments and their personnel. Here appropriate design, good taste and well-trained staff are often the key ingredients to successful experiences. Not always though, the Elbow Room in Vancouver, BC thrived on mild doses of tourist abuse. When regulars would show up behind tourists waiting in line to be seated, they were likely to be told, "You can wait, these boys have to go to work!" The tourists would step aside wondering what hit them and let the regulars be seated. Gunn's last structural component is information and promotion. It is important to provide each tourist market segment with information and promotional materials that create the experience expectation and bring tourists to a destination.

Unfortunately it is this component which has been so badly out of balance in traditional tourism planning to such an extent that resources that should go into training, destination design and physical development have often fallen short. This is less the case now than it was ten to twenty years ago. Another aspect of this component is providing good signage in the destination region to ease and direct movement of people.

Environmental Design Elements

There are three fundamental elements and a series of principles that should figure into a tourism plan. The elements are: local residents, visitors and visitor domain. Too often tourism planners have ignored local residents in their work. Local residents are part of the experience. Their culture contributes to a sense of place, but local residents need privacy as well; they cannot be on show all the time.

Another planning point is that tourism development should occur so that it is accessible to local residents as well as to visitors, that is, development should be affordable and unsegregated. About the visitor, Winterbottom remarks: "The truly successful visitor destination is one that is concerned more with visitor quality than quantity. The quality visitor is the one that is most likely to repeat the visit and to respect the visitor environment-both natural and man made." This statement stands as justification to actively target certain market segments in tourism planning in order to attract desirable visitors and thus conserve advertising dollars for other components of tourism development. The visitor domain is simply an area where attractions and services are clustered so that the tourist experience is aggregated and enhanced.

PRINCIPLES OF TOURISM DEVELOPMENT

Most fundamental design principle is creating the visitor domain with a sense of place that is unique and authentic, and that contains a diversity of potential experience. Reid and Smith encourage development of gateways in designing tourist spaces. The gateway is a physical symbol of entrance to the tourist domain. The gateway also marks the transition from ordinary into extraordinary places and experience. Clustering and concentrating attractions and services is the technique of creating the visitor domain.

Use of these principles leads ultimately to a critical mass of tourist products which establishes a place as a tourist destination in the tourist market. With a critical mass, tourists become aware of the place and will purposely begin to choose to go to that place. The application of the market research technique of product/ market match is the means to achieve a supply of the right tourism products, particularly attractions and services, for the targeted quality tourists of a tourism destination plan. Targeted tourists are statistically defined; the products suitable to their tastes are what should be developed at the destination.

Statistically defined tourist segments usually come from defined geographic areas, fall into specified age and gender groups, have specified education and income levels and have specific preferences for what they like to do, see and eat. Well signed transportation linkages are necessary to ease the movement of people in the tourist domain. Where large crowds of people are concentrated during the tourist season, such as now at the Grand Canyon with four to five million visitors per year, mass transit interventions are rapidly replacing automobile use.

Protecting the environment-natural, cultural and social-is now an accepted mainstay of successful tourism planning. This can be achieved by attracting quality tourists and by managing tourist flows and access while they are in the visitor domain. The Grand Canyon intervention of mass transit is a direct result of the Park Service's goal to protect the environment and preserve the visitor experience. This year Park Service introduced use of a quiet helicopter and will require commercial areal sightseeing operators to use noise-reduced equipment starting next year.

There already are restricted air space regulations. Grand Canyon will be a quieter place soon. The seasons-high, low and shoulder-can be the bane of a tourism planner's life and a test of her skills. In most cases, tourism flows are seasonal but with heavy investment in service and attraction facilities, there is generally a desire by the operators of these facilities to generate year round tourists and thus cash flow. The flip side of this principle is that the seasons with low tourist volumes give local residents periods of reduced stress and rest.

Partnership is another principle to incorporate into successful tourism planning. Because of the pluralistic nature of tourism, there needs to be destination partnerships created or formed which can more effectively take advantage of the product offerings of each member of the partnership. It is the idea of "synergy" where the total is more than the sum of the parts.

Another principle to consider in tourism planning is product life cycle. Tourism products, like many others, grow in popularity and after a while fall off in popularity.

The key is to be prepared when popularity begins to wane and have plans prepared to breathe new life into the attraction or service.

A final principle for successful tourism planning is the planner should insure there is ample opportunity for economic benefits to be captured. Tourists are generally willing to spend money, but as in the Hopi situation, there may be little planned opportunity for them to spend it. For example, most tourists to Hopi are day visitors; they spend money for accommodation in the border towns of Flagstaff, Winslow and Holbrook. There are only a few places to buy food and gas.

Planners are experts, but it takes community vision and community involvement to create a successful tourism plan that reflects the willingness of local residents to go the cost necessary to support tourism in their living space. Murphy provides a comprehensive model for community-based tourism planning. Implementation and action plans are a must in tourism planning because these are the vehicles that create coordination among people and organizations in a destination area.

Without coordination-who is going to do what when with what resources-specified in written or chart form people will forget to do what needs to be done. Monitoring and evaluation are important to measure the success of the plan and to modify it if it is not working out. Successful monitoring depends on establishing a baseline of data from which to measure change. It is unnecessary to measure everything about a plan; select several key indicators and work with those over time.

Scales in Tourism Planning

The range of scale in tourism planning is from site specific physical plans to intermediary community and regional destination plans to national policy plans. No matter at what scale of tourism a planner is working, it is important to incorporate and account for all the components of structure, element, principle and process that have been described. In this way balanced, sustainable tourism development has a chance of being achieved.

Promotion is not Tourism Planning & Development - This misconception has been mentioned several times before, but it is worth reiterating that promotion is only part of successful tourism structure and is only one of four vital components of tourism supply.

Tourism is not an Industry - Tourism is made up of several different indus-tries-aviation, accommodation, food and beverage, attractions-and modes of business enterprise range from a few transnational companies to numerous local small businesses. Government, the public sector, is another major player in tourism development. Governments provide numerous "public good" attractions and conduct or subsidize promotional campaigns of their regions. The nonprofit, volunteer sector also operates attractions of various kinds; most common are county historical museums.

Tourism is not a Smokeless Industry - Tourism can and unfortunately does bring pollution, overcrowding, congestion, destruction of natural and cultural resources, contamination of water supplies, decay of landscapes and vistas with oversized and insensitive physical development and cross cultural clashes in customs and values. Tourism planning must be sensitive to these issues and attempt to anticipate and mitigate the more dire impacts before they develop.

Tourism is the Salvation of Rural & Small Town Economies - Not necessarily! Rural and small towns must have reasonable access to tourist markets and be a special enough place to appeal in order to become successful tourist destinations. Clever rural and small towns see their large urban neighbors, a half hour to an hour driving time away, as their tourist market and they develop attractions and products which interest these people.

For some places, all the boosterism in the world will not overcome an intrinsic lack of natural and cultural resources on which to build a tourism attractions strategy. In other places, there is no distinct sense of place or the authentic and unique have been replaced by homogenized commercial development. In yet other places, local residents do not want tourism development; without local support successful development will be difficult at best.

COMMUNITY-BASED TOURISM PLANNING

The Community-Based Tourism Planning (CBTP) model proposes that tourism planning should build from an awareness of community values and organisational needs to guide more locally-appropriate tourism development that fits with other community needs, initiatives, and opportunities. This brings otherwise established strategic planning and community development principles to tourism planning practices so that stakeholders (residents, operators, government) can together guide a more sustainable and consistent tourism industry for communities, not at the expense of communities and local ecosystems.

There is a growing and more genuine appreciation of the need for increased community involvement in tourism planning to help preserve and maintain unique, special, or valued local features and tourism attractions. Such planning can better prepare a community to "adapt to the unexpected, create the desirable, and avoid the undesirable[and] promotes the opportunity for improving the total community rather than improving one part of the community at the expense of other parts".

Every tourism decision must be made on a community-wide consensus basis. In corporations and institutions, values and visions are commonly clarified at the outset of strategic planning processes and form the basis of short- and long-term decisions and actions. A similar approach can be used as the basis for tourism planning. "Community demands for active participation in the setting of the tourism agenda and its priorities for tourism development and management cannot be ignored".

Though more time-consuming than a top-down approach to planning and development, when a community guides their own development, "the results are often longer lasting and more effective over the long-term". Making and pursuing conscientious and co-operative choices for community development requires patience and perseverance from all stakeholders. Independent operator initiatives, government promotion, and market responses to tourist demands commonly drive tourism development.

Tourism planning, development, and marketing typically focus on tourist trends and desires, thereby insufficiently identifying, upholding, or pursuing the aspirations of affected communities or local residents in a "destination area". All travel is linked with communities no matter how urban or remote the purpose may be. This inescapable fact can be a blessing or a curse depending upon how well a community accepts its tourism role and maintains a balance between traveller and resident development and management.

Rather than "accepting their role", CBTP promotes that the community should define their own-and the tourism industry's-role. To accomplish this, a community needs to create opportunities for stepping back from tourism marketing and product development pressures. Then, stakeholders can evaluate their tourism experiences and local values while setting a direction for their own tourism development in partnership with other significant stakeholders. This community-based approach is fundamentally linked with a "belief in human potential for favorable growth" which relies on community members having a positive view and understanding of their own potential.

CBTP relies on an initial and periodic community assessment process that harnesses the experience, expertise, desires, and support of local residents together with tourism operators and other stakeholders (government, organisations, and industry). Such assessment can generate an inventory of perceptions about tourismrelated changes (experiences, concerns, hopes, fears, and dreams). This "social or perceptual inventory" can complement other tourism resource inventories (infrastructure, services, attractions, biophysical features, and cultural features) for making more informed and accountable decisions while building organisation and infrastructure capacity.

Careful thought and discussion about "what matters to us", "what we can offer", and "how we want tourism to affect our home/community/area" can help to chart a clear course with guiding principles for local tourism planning and development. This process is invaluable when rural, remote, and first nations communities are involved where there are often close communities, shared lands, common resources, and sensitive cultural heritage. Similarly, in more populated destinations, insightful guidance and collaboration can emerge from an assessment process within the many layers or sectors of the community, i.e., "the many communities" affected. Community-based tourism planning is about:

— introducing more "strategic" and "future" thinking or
   visioning to tourism development;

— relying on residents and community leaders as their own "experts" about community needs and desirable tourism influences; and

— providing opportunities to clarify community strengths, challenges, obstacles, and opportunities for social, economic, and ecological well-being.

CBTP encourages and facilitates reflection about how a "destination" is also a "home" (for residents, flora, and fauna). Tourists are more likely to appreciate and return if they feel a "good fit" between aspects of "destination" and "home" rather than experiencing tourism as a source of tension or negative impacts.

This CBTP process model emphasises the need for catalysts from events or individuals to initiate an assessment process, and to keep the process going through tasks that stimulate co-operation, trust, tourism awareness, and links with the broader community development context. The actual "little steps" will vary by community and depend on previous experiences from working or planning together. The success or failure of reducing negative tourism impacts on communities and ecosystems clearly depends on how relationships are valued-relationships between people, and between people and their ecosystems.

The Kyuquot Sound area on the Northwest coast of Vancouver Island is one of the island's last remote coastal tourism destinations, and has one of the most isolated communities of its size. By most accounts, tourism activity is slowly increasing here, but has not yet seriously influenced local planning and development in the community and surrounding wilderness and protected areas.

During Kyuquot's two month peak tourism season in 1997, the four sportfishing lodges, three B&Bs, and one sea kayaking and marine tour company were operating at about 60% of their combined capacity of about 90 clients/

day. There is currently no monitoring of recreational tourist numbers, however, a rough estimate is that commercial tourism accounts for approximately one sixth of visitors to the area. Though not promoted as such, the many provincial protected areas adjacent to Kyuquot Sound are undoubtedly tourism draws.

Tourism is creeping northward on Vancouver Island and the people of Kyuquot are only beginning to more carefully consider its implications and opportunities. In the peak of the summer, there are an estimated 300 seasonal and full-time residents. About two thirds of this population are from the Ka:' yu: 'k' t 'h' (Kyuquot) and Che:k'tles7et'h' (Checleset) First Nation. This is the northernmost band of the Nuuchah-nulth Tribal Council (NTC) which spans most of Vancouver Island's west coast.

Kyuquot's past is generally described as that of a small and remote commercial fishing village that has survived several boom and bust cycles in the whaling and fishing industries during the last 80 years. As in many coastal regions of BC, most local residents are struggling with an almost collapsed local economy that has relied on fishing and forestry.

Assessment

The community assessment provided many tangible and less-tangible outputs from, and for, the many stakeholders. In summary, some tangible tourism planning outputs included:

— A background inventory of tourism planning efforts and dynamics.

— A summary of related influences on the future of tourism.

— A summary of direct, indirect, and potential stakeholders and their roles.

— A set of potential guiding elements for tourism planning.

— A summary of significant hurdles for tourism planning.

— A possible tourism steering group model.

— Initial task suggestions as planning catalysts.

Each of these outputs provides a valuable reference for ongoing tourism-related discussions, organisation, and planning, or for later evaluating the path and successes of tourism planning and development efforts. Some less-tangible community assessment outputs included:

— Encouraging stakeholder awareness about tourism implications and possibilities.

— Identifying shared community and stakeholder interests not otherwise being discussed.

— Demonstrating the collective community wisdom and potential of combining stakeholder input, experience, and expertise.

— Stimulating constructive and cooperative discussions.

— Clarifying relationships and needs.

— Prompting links with other local issues, decisions, and initiatives.

Each of these less-tangible outputs adds to the momentum necessary for stakeholders to begin having a more community-based influence on how tourism affects their lives and the area. Several stakeholders felt that tourismrelated decisions and initiatives could become , opportunities for the community to begin addressing chronic economic, social, and cultural challenges.

Some of these same stakeholders worried that continued haphazard tourism growth could add to economic, social, and cultural conflicts, including lingering tensions between the Native and non-Native local residents. Regardless, awareness is increasing about how tourism is beginning to influence other aspects of community and area well-being.

The most significant assessment outputs were the potential "Guiding Elements" for Kyuquot's tourism planning which came from themes identified through stakeholder comments. With some further discussion, refinement, and community ratification, these can serve as the foundation principles for tourism-related decisions in Kyuquot. These are a starting point for providing more clear and consistent community messages to tourists, tourism operators, government agencies, politicians, and others who influence how tourism affects the community and area.

This helps to demonstrate the comprehensive collective wisdom that can be tapped through a community assessment rather than suggesting or imposing a prescribed list of tourism principles. These stakeholdergenerated Guiding Elements offer more depth and local meaning than what could otherwise be suggested to the community with concepts of eco-or sustainable tourism.

One resident astutely commented that it is much easier to simply make a 2° shift in tourism development directions now, than having to eventually make a 90o shift to change and repair undesired impacts from tourism. This pinpoints the purpose and advantage of identifying guiding elements early in tourism planning. Another resident reflected that, "You have to feel good about your home before you can invite others to it." This is at the heart of community-based tourism planning. Not surprisingly, there are important ways in which all tourism stakeholders can work to support Kyuquot as a healthy home and place to visit.

Several native and non-native residents increasingly avoid or resent tourists who appear to take the community, fishing, and favourite local places for granted. A few residents described their observation that some tourists see the village like an incidental "backdrop for their experience," and not as a living community with real people. Others have had tourists stare at them as though studying "a real Native" like a "monkey in a cage".

These types of encounters and experiences can quickly shatter local confidence, respect, and hospitality in residentvisitor relationships. One Native resident insightfully added that, if local residents increasingly withdraw from contacts with tourists, this will unfortunately only add to the potential for conflicts and stereotyping in both directions, and may subsequently increase tensions within the community. Many described essential links between the "visitor experience" and the "local community experience" whereby each affects the other.

Kyuquot's remoteness, quaint village, local services, sportfishing, secluded beaches, and protected areas are linked to the collective "stakeholder experience" of residents and tourists alike. One tourism operator described hopes that tourists can become more knowledgeable, educated, and inspired from the area and from local people-that tourism can catalyse more meaningful understandings and respect for coastal ecology, remote and rural communities, and Native people.

There was almost a universal stakeholder concern about-and desire to move away from-the status quo of continuing with haphazard, marketdriven, and externally imposed tourism development. Co-operative, inclusive, and community-based tourism planning can be approached as casually or intensively as suits the local context. For Kyuquot, many of the tourism planning "task suggestions" focused on education and training, initiating community co-operation, discussing tourism implications, clarifying community expectations and messages, and stimulating local pride and stewardship.

Given the stakeholder awareness of both desired and negative tourism impacts, there is ample reason to believe that these same stakeholders can prioritise ways of working together to address tourism concerns, and to refine and follow some guiding elements for their own tourism future. "Sustainability", many of the resultant "Guiding Elements" describe an interest in balancing tourism development to "meet the needs of the present without compromising the ability of future generations to meet their own needs". The importance of resident satisfaction for visitor satisfaction. The need to "balance the commercial imperatives of tourism with the cultural integrity of the community".

In tourism planning, issues of sustainability are often linked with other resource and protected area management efforts, especially where protected areas attract visitors. In Kyuquot, many residents have felt alienated from local protected area management. Policies and activities that have emphasised land or marine areas as everyone's resource, playground, or treasure (the "public good" and "provincial interests") typically overlook the greatest potential stewardship asset the local residents. All residents aren't necessarily "connected with the land" or setting stellar examples of treating their home area with care; but if not included in the planning and management, they feel even less of an obligation or need to be stewards.

The community assessment identified the need for tourism and protected area management strategies formed through partnerships between local residents and government agencies. Otherwise, the "tragedy of the commons" remains a tragedy of approaching it as the commons. If tourism and protected area policies are drafted with nobody's home in mind, then nobody in that home is likely to respect, welcome or embrace those policies. Similarly, Kyuquot residents will be reluctant to respect tourists who don't acknowledge that they are visitors or guests to somebody's home area.

It remains to be seen whether the community assessment will stimulate further community-based tourism planning in the Kyuquot area. Nothing more may happen without significant increases in tourism-related pressures and conflicts or without further initiatives from key stakeholders. Nevertheless, stakeholder feedback has been positive about the community assessment contributions to clarifying tourism-related issues and relationships.

The CBTP Process Model (Figure 1) makes the following three assumptions:

— That local capacity building and organisational development can be most effectively guided using the knowledge and insights of stakeholders.

— That most stakeholders can look beyond their immediate circumstance.

— That with community values identified, most stakeholders will move together toward acknowledged desires that respect local area and community well-being.

These assumptions relate to community development and strategic planning principles. Only time and examples of CBTP initiatives elsewhere will provide more insights about the value of this Process Model and validity of its assumptions. A CBTP approach doesn't ignore or preclude more market-conscious tourism planning and development, but first establishes a common framework for shaping a locally appropriate tourism industry.

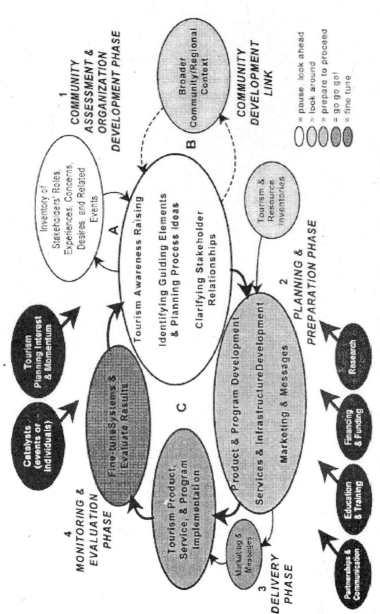

Figure 1. Community-Based Tourism Planning Process Model

In the CBTP Process Model, the three major feedback loops allow for tourism development to be guided and massaged by community, area, and marketconscious inputs. Subsequent assessments could be done after every tourism season, once a year, or at two- or three-year intervals the frequency would depend on the intensity of tourism pressures, other shifts in the local planning context, and stakeholder satisfaction. The specific community approach taken will vary by population size, cultural context, local need, tourism intensity, seasonality, and previous tourism planning efforts. Nevertheless, the CBTP concepts and framework can remain the same. Along the planning path, it is the recipe of individuals-their talents, skills, experience, limitations, commitment, time, patience, and perseverance-which ultimately determines the success of any community-based process.

CHAPTER 2

RESPONSIBILITIES OF TOUR OPERATORS

A tour operator typically combines components to create a holiday. The most common example of a tour operator's product would be a flight on a charter airline plus a transfer from the airport to a hotel and the services of a local representative, all for one price. Niche tour operators may specialise in destinations e.g. Italy, activities e.g. skiing, or a combination. The original raison d'etre of tour operating was the difficulty of making arrangements in far-flung places, with problems of language, currency and communication. The advent of the internet has lead to a rapid increase in self-packaging of holidays, many believe that this trend created serious problems for many tour operators.

Tour operators create, arrange and operate tours and travel programmes, making contracts with hoteliers, airlines and ground transport companies. They market their tours either through travel agencies or directly to customers via websites, digital television and other advertising. They may also arrange for the printing and distribution of brochures advertising the holidays that they have assembled. They are the organisers and providers of package holidays, unlike travel agents, who give advice, sell and administer bookings for tour operators.

The work activities involved will vary according to the size of the tour operator:

— within large tour operators, employees work in a variety of functions, including marketing, IT, public relations, operations, sales and contracts. Tour operators also employ resort representatives within hotels and resorts;

— smaller tour operators employ few staff, who perform a wide range of duties, which will vary according to the time of year.

Many tour operators offer programmes for the summer and winter. Employees can be working at different stages of the annual cycle consecutively, so that in mid summer, they will be confirming the names of customers taking summer holidays, whilst launching their winter programmes.

Typical work activities involve:

— planning which countries and resorts to use, and the number of holidays to offer, using information from previous seasons and market research;

— negotiating with hoteliers, airlines, coach operators and venues to make provisional bookings and agree costs;

— making visits to resorts and accommodation to check its suitability and quality standards;

— preparing brochures/websites, giving information about prices, arranging photographs and descriptions, in compliance with legislation;

— organising the launch of the brochure/website to individual clients and tour operators, with particular emphasis on any new initiatives;

— liaising with airlines and hoteliers to ensure that they can continue to offer the level of agreed service;

— handling bookings received, and forecasting number of holidays sold, making adjustments as necessary;

— liaising with resort representatives, hoteliers, coach operators and airlines;

— organising the issuing of tickets to customers, and invoicing, either directly or via travel agents;

— confirming names of customers to airlines, hotels and overseas staff;

— reviewing the process continually, evaluating customer feedback, and taking action where necessary.

A minority of companies offer salary scales, which reflect entry qualifications. Some roles involving sales offer a basic salary and commission. Salaries vary widely between employers, and depend on the range of duties carried out by the individual and the size of the organisation. Salaries are often higher within business travel companies. Self-employment is also possible, and a number of people establish their own companies, usually after gaining experience with another employer.

Working hours can involve long hours at peak times of year. There is a need to work to tight deadlines, ensure high standards of customer service, and get all the details right, which will mean working additional hours when the pressure is on. Staff are mainly office-based, though some overseas travel may be necessary. Self-employment is possible for those who have experience and contacts within the industry. Part-time work is available at administrative level.

There are limited opportunities to progress within smaller tour operators, though they may offer a broad range of duties and experience. The average profit made on package holidays is very slim. Tour operators have to manage considerable risks, as prices are set over a year before a holiday takes place, and costs can be subject to significant fluctuation, such as exchange rates and airline fuel. This can cause particular stress.

Tour operators range from large international companies to small, specialist tour organisers who organise holidays/travel arrangements for special interest groups, such as sports teams, families, business travellers, those attending language courses and those visiting friends and relatives

TOUR OPERATOR AS TRAVEL AGENT

These people are solely into marketing the concept of travel. They plan and `sell' trips to individuals and groups. They book tickets - for air, rail, sea or road travel, arrange hotel reservations or guest houses, hire taxis etc. Besides domestic, all travel agents undertake international bookings and special business tours or conferences. Tour operators are mostly into travel management. They organise and put together package trips and holidays. These could be for incoming tourists from abroad or outbound tours or even domestic travellers. They can offer special packages, which could include such diverse attractions as deep-sea diving, snorkelling, Himalayan trekking or even camel safaris in the Thar Desert.

Working in this field means dealing with people directly on a daily basis. Helping people plan their itinerary, providing ticketing services to company executives, co-ordinating with the airlines, railways or transport company staff, arranging passports and visas, booking hotels - all these require not only a great deal of mobility but also regular contact with representatives of the various services. One must be up-to-date on rules and regulations governing foreign travel, documents required, hindrances if any; so as to correctly advise the clients. All the staff, be it in marketing, counter sales or guide services must be knowledgeable about the places their clients intend to visit - the best way to reach your destination, places to visit, facilities available etc. Major areas of work in a travel agency include counter work, marketing and management. Counter work involves helping clients with their itineraries, chalking out travel routes, procuring tickets, arranging for passports and visas, making hotel reservations, organising cargo transport and the like.

Counter clerks must be able to have easy access to timetable information and be extremely accurate with the information provided to clients. A small slip on their part could result in embarrassing or even disastrous consequences. Marketing area includes advertising and an aggressive promotion of the agency to potential customers. Procuring steady business for the company is their major job.

The management staff deals with the administration of the agency. The managers co-ordinate and streamline the work of the clerks and select brochures of the various tours and packages available with them, among other things.

ROLES OF A TOUR OPERATOR

— *Planning*: The planning of the tours is done by the tour directors or once-in-a-while by experienced counter clerks. Planning involves chalking out the tour programme, working out the cost, confirmation of accommodation and other facilities like food and entertainment, and consulting tourist officials.

— *Sales and Reservations*: The staff has to ensure that travel brochures are on display at agencies. They also take bookings from travel agents or individuals.

— *Representatives/guides*: These are freelancers mostly whose job involves accompanying tourists to their destination and looking after their needs while travelling. A smattering knowledge of different languages can be useful as well as a general awareness and history of the place visited. This job can be easily do e by students or even office workers and others whc are interested in travelling. Tour operators or local tourism departments often employ professional guides who have a thorough knowledge of the history and cultural significance of a place. Many tour operators, nowadays specialise in areas such as adventure tourism, beach tourism, mountain holidays etc.

— *Entry*: A basic diploma in travel and tourism management can be advantageous to a person seeking to work in this field. Advertisements appear from time to time for jobs available in travel agencies and tour operating companies or for a position in a government department or corporation. In general, the minimum requirement for entry into this industry are: (i) 10+2 and fluency in the spoken language up to tourist guide level. (ii) for higher positions, a graduate degree in any discipline with a specialisation in history and architecture or geography and archaeology can be a great asset as is the knowledge of one or more foreign languages. If one is applying for a government post, he/she has to clear a written test, a personal interview and a medical examination. On-the-job training is provided to all new entrants.

— *Training*: With the demand for trained people increasing by the day, it is wise to gain some insights into the field through professional training. There are a number of institutions in the country which offer training courses on different aspects of the industry. There are equally good correspondence courses too.

— *Career prospects*: A career in travel and tourism can be exciting and full of fun. Not only is it flexible, but certain jobs in the field can provide excellent travelling opportunities. Job prospects include working in: travel agencies as tour operators, in airlines (domestic and foreign) transport and cargo companies, travel consultancy services and in the government run tourism departments. With enough experience and capital, one can even start one's own travel consultancy.

The tourism industry is thus a high-growth industry which can only expand with time, what with more and more people finding the means and the inclination to discover new places and seek new adventures. At the rate the industry is growing, it is certain to be the industry of the 21st century, providing ample job opportunities to all kinds of people at all levels.

CHALLENGES OF TOUR OPERATORS

The tourism industry has been expressing much concern over the five million Indian outbound tourists that are amounting to a revenue outflow of about Rs 25000 crore annually. In an endeavour to divert some of this revenue toward domestic tourism, the industry is all geared up to develop this segment further to give it a much needed thrust. Tour operators have awakened to the fact that domestic tourism is the foundation of strong tourist inflow. With an intent to focus on inter-regional tourism promotion and to boost the potent domestic tourism segment, Indian travel agents and tour operators have for the first time joined hands to aggressively tap this lucrative sector. Until a few years back, India's domestic tourism was limited to only pilgrim tours.

However, today the movement of the domestic market has increased tremendously. This is evident from the fact that even time-share, which till recently was one of the most infamous segments of the industry is now gaining popularity as an easy vacation option. To attract customers, travel agents are now exploring new territories and are sprucing up their itineraries and products. According to the latest travel surveys, there has been a phenomenal rise of ten per cent annual growth in the domestic tourism segment.

The explosion of domestic tourism is an inevitable by-product of economic development in the country. As there is an increase of disposable income, the demand for travel has grown exponentially, diverting most of the traffic toward the outbound segment., putting domestic tourism on the back burner. Where as Indian tourism has been equated with foreign visitors alone or the inbound tourism segment which has been sluggish over the last few years. It is time that India starts equating domestic tourists at par with the foreign tourists to boost its domestic tourism.

Experts believe that Indian tourism has no foundation and lacks projection and awareness. In addition, whenever India has tried to pep up the scenario, several uncalled for events like 9/11, attacks on the parliament and other natural calamities have become major deterrents in the movement of travellers internationally. Weighing the socio-political scenario globally and its adverse impacts on the international movement of both the business and leisure traffic it is only natural that all tour operators have turned focus on domestic tourism, which is both a profitable and feasible proposition in the given scenario. Tour operators are now diverting outbound tourists by enticing them with attractive domestic packages. The industry is now working with various airlines and state tourism departments to work out incentives for the domestic travellers.

To promote domestic tourism, the biggest hurdle has been the inadequate infrastructure. Now the Ministry of

Tourism is becoming aggressive as far as infrastructure development is concerned, development of the tourism circuits is has received a big impetus by the same. While infrastructure development is a continuous process, many agents believe that it is not a burning issue. Tourism experts observe that infrastructure development will take place automatically once there is aggressive movement of tourists.

To strengthen the country's tourism, the geographical diversity can be fruitfully marketed nationally and internationally. This exercise has a lot of significance even regionally. For people in the South, Snow holidays and Himalayas are new attractions and similarly, the beaches and temples of the South can be promoted to the people of North. These products are to be co-ordinated to compete with the attractive packages available for the outbound tourists. Moreover, domestic tourist movement is not limited by seasons, but each season has its own unique selling proposition (USP).

Initiatives like re-introduction of Leave Travel Concession (LTC) are much required to boost domestic tourism. The government's decision to restore the LTC facility to its employees with the hope that the consequential additional outgoing from the exchequer on this account, will at least benefit the tourism industry, has been a welcome decision. Two years ago, the ban on LTC came as a serious blow to the domestic travel agents (since ticket bookings for the employees for the leisure travel generated a good business), depriving them from booking travel tickets for government employees willing to go for leisure tours. LTC has been termed as a good tool to offer a fillip to the leisure travel. The withdrawal of LTC for last two years was counted as an obstacle to the growth of the domestic tourism and was criticised by prominent tour operators. The government employees with the allowance as a disposable income would now be prominent travellers.

In order to create adequate awareness, tourism practitioners point out that media can create the desired hype amongst the populace. Besides, state tourism offices should carry out extensive marketing campaigns jointly with the help of media, tour operators and travel agents, finance companies, hotels and airlines by offering attractive holiday packages to lure the consumers. Due to the lack of publicity, public is unaware of the destinations within the State and outside which are worth seeing and comes under one's budget to spend holidays.

States should organise inter-state Travel Marts/ Exhibitions to expose the tourism potential in their areas. Development of integrated tourist circuits as envisaged in the National Tourism Policy need to be aggressively promoted by the travel trade. This will enable the tourist to visit more than one destination at a given time while planning holidays. Indian Railways can play a major role in this regard by developing special holiday packages for domestic tourists.

TOUR OPERATORS AND PACKAGE TOURS

Tour operators enter into long term contracts with air carriers, hotels and other suppliers for the provision of bulk travel services. Discrete travel services are then assembled into a package tour featuring round trip transportation, seven nights accommodations, ground transportation and tours of local sites. The package tour is marketed to the general public through travel agents. Tour operators are principals and responsible to consumers for the provision of the component travel services of each tour package. Each of these ruined vacations involve a complex marketing system which includes suppliers, both domestic and foreign, wholesalers and tour operators, travel agents and informal travel promoters. Often the negligence of a foreign supplier, i.e., hotel, para-sailing operator, horse or camel stable, tour bus company, air carrier or cruise ship, will be the primary cause of the consumer's injury.

Unfortunately such a potential defendant may be irresponsible, insolvent, uninsured or unavailable because of a lack of jurisdiction or the U.S. forum selected is deemed inconvenient. Assuming availability the potential defendant may be insulated from liability, in whole or in part, because of the application of foreign law, enforceable disclaimers and releases, the Warsaw Convention, U.S. federal and state statutes limiting the liability of cruise ships and hotels and tariffs limiting the liability of carriers. Successful travel litigation depends upon the selection of viable defendants and the application of modern liability theories.

Cooperating air carriers may function as tour operators and be subject to the same theories of liability. For example, an air carrier may own and/or control a captive tour operator. Or the air carrier may be a partner or joint venturer and help finance, organize, operate or market tours to the general public. Air carriers may, however, function as independent contractors entering into arm's length transactions with tour operators. Under these circumstances a cooperating air carrier may be held vicariously liable because of an assumed duty, breach of warranty, apparent authority or third party beneficiary theory. Lastly, the duties and obligations of both tour operators and air carriers may be governed by DOT Public Charter regulations or State travel seller regulations.

As a general rule tour operators may be able to disclaim liability, in the absence of their own negligence, for a consumer's physical injures caused, primarily, by the negligence of a foreign supplier. The traditional theory being that a principal should not be liable for the torts of independent contractors. This general rule can be circumvented by applying one or more of the following theories of liability.

A tour operator may be held liable for the consumer's physical injuries if the tour operator promised, either expressly or implicitly, that the tour would be delivered in a safe and careful manner. Brochure language such as " safe and enjoyable cycling area ", " Marenco's administration and staff work together to make your stay comfortable, safe ", " suitable for handicapped individuals ", " perfectly safe " canoeing conditions and " safe buses " may generate liability under a breach of warranty theory. Alternatively, the tour operator may assume a duty to deliver safe travel services. Assumed duties may more readily overcome written disclaimers than a warranty.

Escorted tours feature close supervision and tour coordination provided by professional tour guides. Older consumers and the parents of students purchase escorted tours. Some sports' tours provide instructors to train and supervise the activities of the participants. In their brochures tour operators will promise that " every tour will be escorted by a qualified professional tour director...carefully selected and trained...informative, they know precisely what you will be seeing and doing...they've been there before "and their " tour escort was a professional and qualified to serve travelers in all matters ". Consumers, especially the parents of students, rely upon promises of close supervision in purchasing such a tour. Consumer injuries caused by the negligence of the tour guide may support claims against the tour operator for negligent selection and supervision of tour guides and misrepresentation of their training, expertise and knowledge of the tour locale.

Tour operators and air carriers may lend their names to promotional brochures giving consumers the impression of ownership and control. When Trans World Airlines describes tours as TWA Getaway tours it is reasonable for consumers to believe that TWA owns, operates, controls and is responsible for the delivery of such tours. When Delta Airlines gives the impression that it is " connected " to Skywest it is reasonable for consumers to believe it is so. When hotel and rental car franchisors fail to distinguish between themselves and foreign franchisees the former may be held liable for the torts of the latter. Describing foreign bus companies, taxi services and ground service providers in possessory terms can generate liability.

Tour operators select the suppliers that will provide the component travel services which make up the package tour. Tour operators should investigate the reliability and willingness of suppliers to deliver safe travel services. Such an investigation should reveal the supplier's financial solvency, prior accident and safety history, the existence of insurance and compliance with all applicable licensing and safety regulations, both domestic and foreign. A failure to conduct such an investigation may generate liability for the negligent selection of suppliers.

Tour operators should design itineraries which maximize safety and minimize the consumer's exposure to risk. Of course, calculated exposure to risk may be a strong selling point in marketing " adventure " tours featuring challenging terrain or white water rafting. Tour operators may be held liable for unnecessarily exposing consumers to risk or designing itineraries in a negligent manner. If tour operators hold themselves out as owning or controlling a foreign service provider then they may be estopped from denying liability for the torts of foreign air carriers, resorts, rental car companies, tour bus companies and other independent contractors. Consumers reasonably rely upon the appearance of ownership and control in purchasing the tour package.

Typically, the injured consumer will be given assistance by the medical staff of the foreign hotel, resort or tour operator. If such medical services are unavailable the consumer may be transported to a recommended foreign doctor, infirmary or hospital. The quality of medical care rendered in foreign locales can exacerbate existing injuries and expose the tour operator to even greater liability. Certainly, domestic carriers have a common law duty to seek proper medical assistance and maintain adequate medical equipment for emergencies. Under an assumed duty theory the tour operator may be obligated to investigate the availability of proper medical care before recommending foreign health care providers.

Identification of the entities involved in marketing and delivering the component elements of the tour is important. Once identified then appropriate legal theories may be developed and applied to each potential defendant. There are situations, however, where the connection between the accident and a viable U.S. defendant is too tenuous to support litigation in a U.S. forum. Under these circumstances it may be necessary to recast the defendants and redefine their marketing function.

Most tour operators recognise that a clean and safe environment is critical to their success. Fewer have the management tools or experience to design and conduct tours that minimise their negative environmental, social and economic impacts while optimising their benefits. To develop and implement these tools in their own operations, and encourage other tour operators to do the same, a group of tour operators from different parts of the world have joined forces to create the Tour Operators' Initiative for Sustainable Tourism Development.

The Initiative is voluntary, non-profit, and open to all tour operators, regardless of their size and geographical location. With this Initiative, tour operators are moving towards sustainable tourism by committing themselves to the concepts of sustainable development as the core of their business activity and to work together through common activities to promote and disseminate methods and practices compatible with sustainable development.

The Initiative has been developed by tour operators for tour operators with the support of the United Nations Environment Programme (UNEP), the United Nations Educational, Scientific and Cultural Organization (UNESCO) and the World Tourism Organization (WTO/ OMT), who are also full members of the Initiative. Under this international umbrella, tour operators who are members of the Initiative will be able to respond to international agendas while creating a platform to develop ideas and projects to address the environmental, social, economic and cultural aspects of sustainable development within the tourism sector.

In particular, the members of the Initiative have formed Working Groups in four key areas of action:

— Sustainability Reporting
— Cooperation with destinations
— Supply Chain Management
— Communication

Tour Operators' Performance Indicators

The Tour Operators' Initiative, in cooperation with the Global Reporting Initiative (GRI), has developed a Sector Supplement to the GRI 2002 Sustainability Reporting Guidelines providing Tour Operators' performance indicators. Forty-seven indicators have been developed to measure tour operators' performance in addressing the environmental, economic and social impacts of their business operations.

The tour operators' supplement adds to, but does not replace, the 2002 GRI Sustainability Reporting Guidelines' section on performance indicators. The tour operator's sector supplement applies only to businesses dedicated to organizing holiday packages, that is a pre-arranged combination of accommodation, transport and other tourism services not ancillary to transport or accommodation and accounting for a significant proportion of the package, when the service covers a period of more than twenty-four hours or includes overnight accommodation.

The supplement was not designed to capture sector-specific aspects of the various service industries associated with a package, such as transport, accommodation, and other tourism services. The tour operator's performance indicators are divided into categories that reflect the life cycle of the holiday product: from the planning stage, to the development and delivery of the product. The indicators have been grouped under five categories:

— *Product management and development (PMD)* includes actions related to the choice of the destination as well as the type of services to be included (e.g., the use of train vs. plane).

— *Internal management (IM)* reflects all the operations and activities that take place in the headquarters or country offices (e.g., use of office supplies, production of brochures, direct employment).

— *Supply chain management (SCM)* addresses actions related to the selection and contracting of service providers.

— *Customer relations (CR)* summarises the actions taken to deal with customers, not only with regards to the responsibility to serve them and reply to their comments, but also the opportunity to provide information and raise consumer awareness regarding sustainability.

— *Cooperation with destination (D)* includes all activities and decisions related to destinations that tour operators make beyond the production and delivery of their holiday package. This mainly includes efforts made by tour operators to engage in dialogues with destination operators about the impacts of tour packages, and philanthropic activities.

During the process of developing the supplement, the participants began to develop 'guidance notes' listing recommended best practices, as well as more specific instructions on the sustainability issues to be taken into account for three specific indicators. The guidance notes have not been officially reviewed and approved as part of the GRI framework and represent the experience and recommendations of the TOI and the members of the Multi Stakeholders Working Group.

The Tour Operators' Initiative (TOI) entered, in Summer 2001, an official agreement with the Global Reporting Initiative (GRI), to produce the tour operator's specific supplement to the GRI 2002 Sustainability Reporting Guidelines. A key element of the agreement was the recognition that the tour operator specific supplement will be developed in full consultation with all the relevant stakeholders. Key stakeholders' representatives were then selected in consultation with relevant experts, and a Multi-Stakeholder Working Group (MSWG) was established.

The Multi Stakeholder Working Group included twelve tour operators members of the Tour Operators' Initiative, as well as representatives from Non Governmental Organizations, trade unions, tourism board, local authorities, tour operators' suppliers, consumers' associations, from various regions of the world. The tour operator's sustainability reporting performance indicators were developed according to the following work plan:

— *Step 1*: preparation - by the members of the MSWG - of First Draft of the sustainability reporting performance indicators for the selected areas of activity/impact.

— *Step 2*: First Draft of the Tour Operators' Sustainability Reporting Performance Indicators - addressing internal and supply chain management and customers' awareness - posted on the web for public comments, and sent to key stakeholders and organizations for targeted comments.

— *Step 3*: Second Draft of the Tour Operators' Sustainability Reporting Performance Indicators prepared by the MSWG, accounting also for external comments received in Step 2. This Second draft prepared during the second Multi Stakeholder Working Group Meeting will also include an additional set of indicators addressing tour operators' impacts and influence on destinations.

— *Step 4*: Second Draft of the Tour Operators' Sustainability Reporting Performance Indicators - addressing internal and supply chain management, customers' awareness and activities at destinations - posted on the web for public comments, and sent to key stakeholders and organizations for targeted comments.

— *Step 5*: Third and Final Draft (PDF 40kb) of the Tour Operators' Sustainability Reporting Performance Indicators finalised by the MSWG, accounting also for external comments received in Step 4.

— *Step 6*: preparation by the MSWG of the vision paper: how the performance indicators will be further developed in the following years.

— *Step 7*: submission of the final draft of the Tour Operator's sector performance indicators to the GRI Board of Directors for approval.

— *Step 8*: Approval by the GRI Board in September 2002 and publication of the Tour Operator's as a supplement to the updated GRI 2002 Sustainability Reporting Guidelines by mid-2002.

The members of the Tour Operators' Initiative will participate in a pilot phase in 2003, the main objectives of which are to build awareness and know-how on reporting principles and practices, and to facilitate the revisions and improvement of the indicators, through the generation of the following outputs:

— A user's manual containing guidance notes to a number of indicators based on collected best practices, as well as measuring protocols.

— Recommendations on most effective reporting formats for the sector.

— A proposed model suitable to the tour operators' sector for organising the internal flow of information to support reporting efforts.

— Recommendations of the links between the core 2002 Guidelines and tour operator-specific indicators.

— A proposed classification of core and advanced indicators for the tour operators' sector.

The pilot will not only provide the structure for tour operators to learn about Sustainability Reporting and the Tour Operators' Performance Indicators, but also the platform to revise the indicators based on a better understanding of their business and sustainability relevance. Most participants indicated that the tour operator's sector supplement should be reviewed in two- to three years' time.

Integrating sustainability into tour operators' business practices: Effectively integrating sustainability into the tour operators' business means considering environmental, social and economic aspects throughout the process of developing a holiday package. The key operating areas where tour operators can integrate sustainability practices are:

— Internal management, by taking into account sustainability principles in the management of human resources, office supplies and production of printed materials;

— Product development and management, by planning tours and selecting holiday package components that minimise environmental, economic and social impacts;

— Contracting with suppliers, by integrating sustainability principles into the selection criteria and service agreements of suppliers;

— Customer relations, by guaranteeing privacy, health and safety standards, and providing customers with information on responsible behaviour and sustainability issues at their destinations; and

— Relations with destinations, by supporting destination stakeholders' efforts to address sustainability issues and proactively contributing to conservation and development projects.

Moreover, to ensure that activities targeted toward sustainability are comprehensive, credible and lead to long-term positive changes, it is important to integrate sustainability principles into corporate policy and management systems, and to monitor and report on performance.

Responses by individual tour operators in each of these areas vary considerably, influenced by their size, type of holiday packages offered and destinations served. Since the launch of the Tour Operators' Initiative in 2000, the TOI Secretariat has been collecting from the individual members 'good' examples of how a tour operator can effectively integrate the principles of sustainability into its various areas of operations. This effort has been very successful, not only because it demonstrates that the members of the TOI actually take

action, but, most importantly, because it helps spread
awareness that tour operators can actually do something
about sustainability.

SUPPLY CHAIN ENGAGEMENT

A wide range of possible actions that tour operators can
take, each company should select the actions that are
most appropriate to its organization and the types of
destinations and suppliers with which it works. It is not
necessary to try to implement all the actions at once;
indeed, it is often better to start with a few achievable
actions and then build on those in the future. What is
important is that a company start to take action. As
intermediaries between tourists and tourism service
providers, tour operators bring together a variety of
tourism-related services to form a complete holiday
package, which is then marketed to customers either
directly or through travel agents. Each package generally
consists of accommodation, transport both to and from
the destination, ground transport within the destination,
and events or activities such as excursions and social
activities.

Because most of the goods and services included in a
holiday package are provided by a supply chain of
subcontracted companies, organizations and agents, tour
operators are not always in direct control of the
environmental and social impacts of those products. Yet,
consumers increasingly expect the companies they buy
from to ensure that their products provide not just quality
and value-for-money, but also safeguard environmental
and social sustainability. Companies must take
responsibility for ensuring the sustainability of all the
inputs that go into their products. For tour operators,
who offer products comprised almost entirely of
contracted goods and services, this means that effectively
implementing sustainability policies requires working

closely with suppliers to improve sustainability performance in all the components of a holiday - throughout the life cycle of a holiday package.

Consumers are increasingly interested in the world behind the product they buy. Life cycle thinking implies that everyone in the whole chain of a product's life cycle, from cradle to grave, has a responsibility and a role to play, taking into account all the relevant external effects. The actions presented are applicable to tour operators of any size, from the smallest to the largest. Although the way each company is organized can differ - thus affecting the staff who will need to be involved in various actions - here outlines the different roles that need to be brought together to develop and implement a sustainable supply chain policy and action plan.

Developing Sustainable Supply Chain

Working with suppliers to integrate sustainability into the supply chain can benefit tour operators, suppliers, customers and destinations. From a financial standpoint, improved sustainability can lower costs through greater operating efficiency, reduced waste generation, and reduced consumption of energy and water. Sustainability practices can also lead to increased revenue and shareholder value by generating more repeat business and attracting new business from customers who value good environmental and social performance. A strong positive reputation as a company that cares about sustainability issues, coupled with improvements to the quality of the tourism experience provided to clients, can result in increased customer satisfaction and loyalty, strengthened brand value, enhanced publicity and marketing opportunities, and better acceptance by local communities in destinations. Good performance and a high-quality, sustainable product can also help a tour operator reduce the risk of conflict or problems with suppliers, governments, staff and local communities, and improve its status as a respected partner in destinations.

This may mean enhanced access to key business resources such as capital, the ability to develop products to meet growing market demand, improved relationships with governments, and a motivated and loyal staff. The costs and benefits of integrating sustainability criteria into the supply chain will vary for each company, depending on:

— Purchasing and contracting arrangements with suppliers;

— Availability of alternate suppliers in key destinations;

— Suppliers' current levels of sustainability performance and potential for change;

— Barriers to sustainability, such as external factors;

— A company's main sustainability and operational concerns; and

— Resources available to implement and promote sustainability throughout the supply chain.

Supply Chain Policy

For a tour operator, effectively integrating sustainability into its supply chain will require the establishment of a coherent company policy and accompanying management system that set out clear targets and actions on economic, environmental and social performance. Building this system on already existing internal processes will help keep down the costs of implementation and promote integration within a company's overall operations.

To establish this policy, a company needs to conduct a baseline assessment of its tourism service suppliers' current performance on sustainability, in order to determine priority targets and actions. The management system should include procedures for monitoring, reviewing and reporting on progress made in integrating sustainability principles into the company's supply chain. This helps to ensure transparency and allow tour operators to adapt any policies or actions that are not achieving their sta ?d goals. Progress can be measured against the initial l iseline assessment.

Create A Policy

Goal

Develop a coherent policy for improving the economic, environmental and social sustainability performance of suppliers, and for integrating it into existing company management systems.

Actions

— Build a team to develop and implement the policy

  — Bring together representatives of each area or department in the company that may have a role in implementing the overall policy, or which may be affected by it.

  — Create a management team to develop and implement the policy at each stage, drawing on expertise from all departments.

  — Consider inviting your company's suppliers to participate in the policy and planning process.

— Assess the company's strengths and opportunities

  — Assess the company's current position and policies and how they relate to sustainability issues.

  — Consider trends and potential developments, including product quality, supplier performance and markets, as well as the way the company interacts with its suppliers.

— Identify opportunities to improve the sustainability performance of suppliers.

— Develop a policy

   — Elaborate a common vision that can be shared by all departments in the company, based on the results of the strengths and opportunities assessment.

   — Discuss the common vision with key staff, and invite their suggestions for policies and actions to implement this vision.

   — Based on these discussions and the common vision, develop and agree on a policy and strategic goals for improved supply chain sustainability, and on the types of methods that could be used to meet these goals.

Baseline Assessment of Suppliers

Goal

Assess suppliers' current sustainability performance and their strengths and weaknesses, to generate data for designing a sustainability action plan, and to provide a baseline against which to measure progress over time and review and modify the sustainable supply chain policy and actions.

Actions

— Prepare an approach for assessment

   — Develop assessment tools for measuring the sustainability performance of suppliers.

   — Select a sample of suppliers to involve in the assessment.

   — Consider prioritizing certain supplier groups, based on ability to influence them and the ease of addressing any identified impacts. Trying to

> tackle every type of service and every supplier or contractor at the same time can be very resource intensive.

— Assess suppliers' current performance

> — Use questionnaires, personal meetings and/or workshops to assess suppliers' current sustainability performance, strengths and weaknesses, their main concerns and the key areas requiring improvement.

> — Determine suppliers' general levels of awareness, technical capacity and desire to be involved in a sustainability program. In particular, it is important to understand their motives and values, and to identify any potential challenges or barriers to sustainability.

> — Identify any opportunities for additional cooperation with external stakeholders, in particular local authorities or NGOs.

> — Ask suppliers for information on how they select their own suppliers. They may already implement a range of good practices, such as buying food from local producers and organic and/or fair trade suppliers.

Prepare an Action Plan

Goal

Prepare an action plan for implementation of policies for improving the economic, environmental and social sustainability performance of suppliers, taking into account suppliers' strengths and weaknesses and existing company management systems.

Actions

— Define actions and set targets

- Define and agree on actions and targets to be achieved, based on the company's sustainable supply chain policy.
- Ensure that targets are SMART (Specific, Measurable, Achievable, Realistic and Time-specific).
- Set standards by which to measure suppliers' performance.
- Ensure that standards are achievable. It is better to set standards that are achievable and can provide real satisfaction for suppliers and staff, rather than set over-ambitious standards that are unlikely to be achieved.
- Develop an action plan to implement the strategy and meet set targets
- Agree on specific responsibilities for each department and the resources they will need to implement them, such as training or technical information. Incorporate departmental action plans in regular company procedures for reviewing progress and staff appraisal.
- Prepare a timetable for implementation of the overall plan and for each individual action.
- Get the word out
  - Inform suppliers about the sustainability policy and action plan, and the benefits of improved environmental, social and economic performance, through normal company communication channels, dedicated workshops and personal meetings between suppliers and company representatives.
  - Inform staff about the sustainability policy and action plan through training workshops, briefings and feedback materials, and internal capacity-

building on how to raise awareness of the policy and provide support to suppliers.

— Establish a system to keep staff informed of progress, for example through staff newsletters and the intranet.

— Put the plan into action

— Consider prioritizing suppliers for involvement in the first stages of the program, based on economic and managerial considerations. It may be more practical to begin with just a few destinations and/or selected suppliers, rather than trying to introduce the program everywhere at once.

— Recognize that suppliers may have different priorities for improvements and are likely to make progress at different rates.

— Understand that change takes time. It is important to focus on achieving continuous improvements, rather than trying to achieve everything all at once. The key is to initiate programs with all suppliers to improve their performance and see measurable improvement over time.

— Consider working with other partners, including public authorities, NGOs and other tour operators operating in the same destination, to help encourage sustainability performance improvements amongst all suppliers, for example by developing a common approach in certain geographic or supplier areas.

Monitor and Report on Progress

Goal

Monitor and report on progress made in integrating sustainability into the company's supply chain, to ensure that goals have been achieved and to identify any potential problems.

Actions

— Create and implement a monitoring system

    — Select appropriate indicators for monitoring performance.

    — Hold regular meetings with relevant individuals, to review progress and help sort out problems as they arise. Key staff in each area often understand best where and how improvements can be made, and involving them in the process helps to build and maintain their commitment to sustainability.

    — Ensure that monitoring is frequent enough to detect problems at an early stage, so that corrective action can be taken if needed.

    — Identify and refine the most successful approaches to improvement of sustainability performance across the company's supply chain.

    — Store information collected through monitoring in a central database.

    — Learn from successes and difficulties in implementing planned actions and modify plans accordingly; use the results of a progress review to plan for the year ahead.

— Report on performance

    — Report internally by communicating the results of monitoring back to staff, to show what has been achieved, recognize their commitment to the project and remind them of the program's objectives and targets.

    — Agree on the format for a public report on supply chain sustainability, for example as a separate report or a section of the company's annual report.

— Consider using a third party to review the company's sustainability report before publication.

— Disseminate regular reports on progress to demonstrate a commitment to improving overall sustainability performance in the supply chain to key stakeholder groups, including suppliers, staff, customers, media, destinations and others in the tourism industry. Reporting also helps to foster openness and discussion about problems and successes and enables companies to more effectively prioritize future activities.

Sustainability Goals

Tour operators are well-placed to support suppliers in improving their economic, environmental and social performance. As tour operators interact directly with potential customers, they understand their clients' growing demands for high quality and sustainability. They also often have access to technology and information that smaller suppliers may have difficulty obtaining on their own. Because tour operators deal with a wide range of different suppliers, they can more easily gather information on a variety of best practices and facilitate the sharing of experiences amongst suppliers.

There are a number of ways that tour operators can enable their suppliers to improve their sustainability performance and meet set sustainability criteria and targets. Three of these measures - awareness raising, technical support and the provision of incentives. The appropriate mix of support measures for each company and supplier will depend on the results of the baseline assessment and the approach that the company has chosen to adopt for implementing its sustainable supply chain strategy.

Awareness on Sustainability Issues

Goal

Raise awareness amongst suppliers on relevant sustainability issues and demonstrate why sustainability performance is important.

Actions

— Develop awareness-raising messages on sustainability

  — Take into account feedback from suppliers, existing relationships with targeted supplier groups, the level of interest amongst suppliers in participating in the program, and suppliers' current capacity and priorities for performance improvement.

  — Design messages based on the dissemination channels that will be used to raise awareness, such as mailings, personal visits, workshops, etc.

  — Identify potential partners and support. Local partners, such as business associations or training institutes, can help open communication channels with local suppliers, especially amongst smaller enterprises, and may be influential in reinforcing awareness-raising efforts.

  — Focus on key issues that are important to the company's situation and its suppliers.

  — Provide information in the awareness-raising materials on the overall strategy and time frame for the company's sustainability program.

— Communicate sustainability messages to suppliers

  — Identify the characteristics of each group of suppliers, including their values and concerns, and select appropriate tools, media and styles to best reach these target groups. Tools might include workshops, bilateral meetings or dialogues, briefing materials and feedback forms for staff, checklists and questionnaires, or printed materials, such as leaflets, posters and manuals.

— If questionnaires or checklists are used, indicate clearly what the information gathered would be used for. Consider preparing a summary report on the results, for example highlighting sustainability issues identified as priorities by suppliers and illustrating the general level of performance for each of the issues addressed.

— Use personal communication wherever possible. Staff in contact with suppliers can provide up-to-date information on sustainability issues and the company's progress. Trained staff should be available to inform suppliers about environmental and social issues, provide contact phone numbers, make personal visits, etc.

— Ensure that sustainability issues are followed up and discussed regularly with suppliers. Encourage feedback from suppliers to help evaluate the effectiveness of awareness-raising activities and provide important information on the attitudes of target groups to sustainability issues. This feedback can be used to refine awareness-raising activities and plan future developments.

— Monitor the response to the awareness-raising actions. Check how suppliers and staff respond to the project, recognize and appreciate results, and support continuous improvement. A newsletter may be a good way to publicize examples of good practice and progress made by particular suppliers.

Provide Technical Support

Goal

Support suppliers in improving their sustainability performance, particularly in areas that have been identified as priorities.

Actions

— Assess where support is needed

  — Determine where technical support is needed amongst suppliers and establish targets for improvement.

  — Identify the most appropriate technical support and capacity-building actions to match the suppliers' and company's targets.

— Develop and deliver support

  — Identify, develop and deliver the most appropriate and effective technical support tools for suppliers, including printed material, workshops, bilateral meetings or dialogues, briefing materials and feedback forms for staff, training sessions, checklists and questionnaires, and telephone and on-line information and support services.

  — Provide training and practical education opportunities to suppliers' staff at all levels, including managers, engineers, hotel maids, catering staff, guides, etc., on reducing resource use and procedures for waste separation and recycling.

  — Offer links to networks of local, national and international advisers on sustainability and business issues who can provide on-line and on-site assistance to suppliers - for example local experts on environmental and socio-economic issues, possibly in collaboration with local trade associations and non-governmental organizations.

— Consider promoting the use of eco-labeling schemes to support improvement and provide information on technical issues tailored to a specific destination.

— Identify external sources of information and support. Numerous technical materials on environmental management and solutions are already available through international and national hotel associations, international organizations and NGOs.

— Arranging for suppliers to contact these sources directly can help such organizations disseminate their resources more widely and avoid overwhelming an internal team with requests for information and support, which might be difficult to meet with limited internal resources.

Incentives to Sustainable Suppliers

Goal

Build support for the sustainable supply chain strategy by recognizing and rewarding suppliers for improvements on key environmental, social and economic issues.

Actions

— Create an incentive scheme

— Establish sustainability performance standards for the sustainability priorities set by the company's policy, to identify which suppliers will be offered additional promotional opportunities and/or other incentives.

— Identify the most suitable incentive measures to reward suppliers making significant improvements, such as preferential contracting, promotional opportunities, awards and events, for example:

— Indicate that suppliers who demonstrate improved performance will be the company's first choice when decisions are made on whom to contract in any destination or category. Preferential contracting offers a major incentive to suppliers to improve their performance.

— Highlight good performers in catalogs and brochures with a special logo, making sure to provide clear information to customers about what the logo denotes.

— List specific sustainability actions that each supplier has adopted in the catalogs.

— Present certificates to suppliers who demonstrate the best sustainability performance.

— Organize events - in a destination or at company headquarters - for groups of suppliers who are making good progress in implementing sustainability performance improvements.

— Develop and agree on the internal procedures for providing the identified additional promotional opportunities and incentives.

— Get the word out

— Inform suppliers about additional promotional opportunities and other incentives and the criteria that the company will use to allocate them.

— Ensure that available recognition and reward opportunities and incentives are discussed with each supplier in personal meetings with a company representative.

— Verify supplier performance

— Define mechanisms for collection of data on suppliers' performance in the identified action areas, such as questionnaires, personal visits, etc., and train staff to implement these procedures.

— Create a monitoring and assessment system and procedures to verify suppliers' declared sustainability performance.

— Establish a database to record information on suppliers' sustainability performance and ensure that the database can be easily used by all staff who need to access the information it will hold. Where appropriate, integrate the database with existing systems, such as health and safety databases.

Integrate Sustainability Criteria

Full integration of sustainability issues into a tour operator's business practices will require alterations to the way purchasing choices are made and suppliers' contracts are written. Inclusion of sustainability criteria in suppliers' contracts highlights the importance of sustainability issues to the tour operator's core business and ensures that priority issues are addressed with suppliers from the start.

Sustainability criteria can be incorporated into suppliers' contracts to set both minimum performance standards that all suppliers of a particular type must meet and further optional criteria that they are encouraged to achieve. Performance against sustainability criteria will need to be monitored and assessed as part of regular reviews of suppliers.

Goal

Integrate environmental, social and economic criteria into suppliers' contracts and reward performance improvements by preferentially contracting suppliers that meet those criteria.

Actions

— Set sustainability contracting standards

  — Establish the minimum sustainability performance standards to be included in suppliers' contracts, and link them to the performance standards set as part of an incentive scheme.

  — Set standards sufficiently high so that they represent good performance and real improvements, but also ensure that they will be realistic and achievable for suppliers.

  — Allow flexibility to accommodate varying local socio-economic and environmental conditions among different destinations and different types and sizes of suppliers.

  — Seek guidance on standards for different types of suppliers from relevant national or international bodies.

  — For each destination, review the sustainability performance of the full range of suppliers for each service or item and identify alternate supply options.

— Set a sustainable contracting system

  — Develop and agree on an internal approach and procedures for implementation of sustainability performance as a contracting criteria.

  — Draft contractual clauses to reflect minimum performance requirements on key issues and consider legal matters arising from incorporation of sustainability standards into suppliers' contracts.

  — Establish procedures to deal with suppliers that fail to meet minimum set standards or that have submitted false information. In serious cases and on specific issues, companies may decide to suspend contracts with suppliers who are in breach of contract conditions.

— Consider appointing an individual staff member or a small team to develop and update standards and support materials, coordinate training for suppliers and staff, manage informational databases, coordinate monitoring, auditing and verification, and provide progress reports.

— Get the word out

— Run workshops to train staff on contracting procedures for sustainability issues and procedures for monitoring and auditing suppliers' sustainability performance.

— Set up a communications program to inform suppliers about the new contract clauses and contracting policy.

— Consider developing a parallel voluntary program with additional sustainability performance standards.

— Offer assistance to help get suppliers back into compliance, for example by making suggestions for improvements and sources of technical assistance.

— Monitor and evaluate the system

— Set up assessment and monitoring procedures to evaluate supplier sustainability performance in relation to standards set in contracts. For example, arrangements could be made for sustainability performance to be audited as part of existing health and safety audits.

— Arrange for this assessment and monitoring to be conducted by the supplier, the company or a third party, using checklists, questionnaires, site visits and staff interviews as appropriate. Customer feedback through surveys or informal comments can also be an important source of information.

— Establish a database to record information on suppliers' sustainability performance and ensure that the database can be easily used by all staff who need to access the information it will hold. Where appropriate, integrate the database with existing systems, such as health and safety databases.

— Ensure the confidentiality of any sensitive or confidential data in the database.

CHAPTER 3

PROMOTING DESTINATIONS

A tourist destination is a city, town or other area the economy of which is dependent to a significant extent on the revenues accruing from Tourism. It may contain one or more tourist attractions or visitor attractions and possibly some "Tourist traps". Natural attractions draw visitors to see what the world was like before tourism left previous, traditional cultures abandoned, as Western influence swept the world. Popular Cities such as London, New York City, Sydney, Paris, Toronto, Rome, and Tokyo have a large number of tourists each year, making them a huge tourist site.

Promotion is an important part of any tourism program. For ecotourism and nature-based tourism programs, certain factors need to be considered before any promotion begins. Specifically, the fragility of the sites that tourists will be visiting, the impacts that visitor use will have on the area, and the level of visitation that can be sustained without harming the area need to be identified. For example, areas hig'hly impacted by even a small degree of visitor use should either be not promoted at all or promoted to an extremely limited degree. Word-of-mouth advertising often attracts enough visitors to these areas already, making additional promotion unnecessary. Areas that can handle a larger number of visitors without being negatively impacted can be promoted to a greater extent.

Certain types of tourism fit a site's goals and objectives better than others. As with any management action, promotional campaigns should reflect the site's stated policy vision statement and objectives. For example, at natural sites, if local economic development is an objective, managers may wish to promote bird-watching or trekking where local people may be hired as guides or drivers. At an archaeological site affected by theft of objects destined for trafficking in stolen art, a promotional programme may be designed to attract better-off visitors who are willing to pay an extra fee to support an artisan cooperative making high-quality replicas of objects at the site. These can then be sold to satisfy a portion of the demand fed by trafficking. The segmentation process requires research into the characteristics and preferences of visitors who may want to come to a site. Distinct segments of consumers might include those belonging to museum associations or organisations for the protection of wildlife. Identifying people with similar motivations and needs enables the manager to pinpoint the types of promotional materials needed. A simple example is an elderly target audience, for whom promotional materials can be in larger print and may list special services for senior citizens.

To be selected for management action, a market segment must have three characteristics:

— it must be measurable,

— it should be easy to reach through promotional distribution systems, and

— it should promise increased earnings sufficient to more than repay the costs of targeting it with promotional materials.

Knowing how tourists inform themselves on a site they wish to visit will help identify where to focus promotional efforts: For example, since most "eco-tourists" wishing to see polar bears in Manitoba, Canada, seek information from travel agents, the site's managers are wise to send their promotional materials to travel agencies. However, since few travel agencies are able or willing to stock the full range of available brochures and are ill-prepared to deal with specialised inquiries, a more efficient approach may be to send agents a brochure and then contact them personally to brief them on the site's attractions and the logistics of reaching it.

Developing a theme using a site's central message for the park's promotion helps develop marketing and promotional materials. Combining a site's most attractive elements to develop slogans or "soundbites", will facilitate the design and creation of brochures and interpretation displays. For instance, a park could be "the best kept secret in the Caribbean", or the place where "billions of years of nature meet thousands of years of history".

An analysis of strengths, weaknesses, opportunities and threats (SWOT) can be used to identify gaps between a site's promotion strategy and tourism trends. A SWOT analysis is a marketing tool used to evaluate a site's promotional abilities by examining the strengths and weaknesses of its promotional organisation, financial and staff resources, and existing promotional strategy. Strengths and weaknesses are considered factors over which the site has some control; opportunities and threats are external. Strengths and weaknesses include:

— the ways in which the site is being marketed, the size of the marketing budget, performance measures and the degree and nature of the staff's involvement in marketing efforts

— the site's tourism products, including the quality of service, image and reputation

— a profile of current visitors

— suppliers and the quality of goods and services they provide

— the people who handle any marketing for the site and the image they promote, for example, the way it is presented by tour operators compared with the site's own promotional materials.

— political factors, including government legislation

— economic factors

— social factors

— competition, identifying competitors and analysing their strengths and weaknesses

Managers without sufficient time or staff to carry out promotional tasks may consider seeking outside assistance. Tasks such as writing to guidebook publishers, magazines and newspapers to publicise attractions and present management issues are time-consuming and vie for a manager's attention. An independent promotional organisation representing the different interest groups may provide a solution. Such a group can analyse a site's tourism market and management realities. It has the further virtue of being independent, so that it can bridge gaps between competing interest groups.

A group such as an NGO with ties to the site and that knows the tourism business, or a government group with a mandate to coordinate all the stakeholders could play this role. An independent organisation set up to facilitate tourism and park promotion at Lake Baikal, Russia, produced a guidebook giving the names of local tour operators and guides, and distributed it in North America, Europe and Japan. If an outside organisation is solicited, it must be given clear direction so that its output reflects the site's goals and objectives. For example, if a goal is to support local entrepreneurs, such as ground operators, the organisation must ensure that it promotes both smaller local operators as well as larger or regional and national companies.

Developing a site's "tourism identity" is an essential element of a promotional strategy. This identity, which is based on the site's goals, objectives and market potential, becomes associated with the site in the minds of potential visitors. It could centre on a famous fresco or an endangered animal, for example, and be used to develop a logo for future promotional activities.

SITE PROMOTION STRATEGIES

International tourist guidebooks can be a free source of promotion. Guidebooks are a popular source of information for trip planning and are available for almost every country and region of the world. Because guidebook information is constantly changing, new editions are regularly updated, and editors are usually willing to publish information free of charge. This presents an opportunity to have information on a site and local attractions and services distributed to a wide audience.

Supplying information to travel magazines, newspapers, radio and the internet is another costeffective way to promote a site. Travel magazines and newspapers publish information on tourism attractions free of charge and local radio and television stations broadcast such information as a public service. These can all be useful sources of free publicity for the site. In-flight airline magazines reach a large public, and because they are published quarterly or bimonthly, articles remain in circulation for considerable periods. Most publications can be accessed by the internet and the information transferred in this manner.

Brochures can be used to distribute site information to a wide range of audiences. They can be mailed to national tourism offices, included in promotional information sent to tour operators, newspapers, magazines, radio and television stations and distributed to hotels. However, unlike other types of promotional material, brochures are costly to produce, and should be designed to remain valid over a long period of time. Most people who receive brochures read them. However, research has found that brochures are likely to exert more influence on people who have not visited a site before and less likely to attract repeat visitors.

Contacting tour operators directly is a useful means of interesting them in a site. Tour operators are always on the lookout for new attractions to sell to their clients. Operators, particularly companies that specialise in activities offered at the site, will appreciate receiving a brochure and any information about the local community. Direct contact with tour operators bypasses travel agencies and improves the chances of a positive response.

Producing an information package to area attractions and services can help direct benefits to local residents. If one of the goals of a site's tourism programme is to benefit local communities, a multi-lingual community guide sheet may be a valuable promotional tool. It can direct visitors to neighbouring destinations and attractions, providing a detailed picture of what the area offers, including dining, shopping and accommodations. The information is especially useful for attracting the independent traveller. Such a package should be distributed to key points such as hotels in major cities and at national tourism offices or embassies abroad. If a site has internet, it can be distributed electronically. A guide can also be used as a management tool for bringing about desired visitor behaviour, by for example discussing cultural rules and taboos and good conservation practices. Such a guide can be produced by the community with the help of site management. A local NGO may provide free computer time and translating services. Selling the guide even if it is very simple may help pay for future copying expenses.

National tourism offices or embassies can be a free and effective means of distributing promotional materials. Tour operators are always on the lookout for new attractions to sell to their clients. Operators, particularly companies that specialise in activities offered at the site, will appreciate receiving a brochure and any information about the local community. Direct contact with tour operators bypasses travel agencies and improves the chances of a positive response.

Holding a press day can be an effective way to introduce a site to the media. The day can be scheduled to coincide with a cultural celebration at the site, or it could be a yearly event held to mark the beginning of the tourist season. Tour operators, hotel owners and government officials who belong to the site's advisory group can be recruited to play a role. These stakeholders usually have press contacts and may be interested in obtaining media coverage of their activities or businesses. National tourist offices sometimes organise familiarisation tours for travel writers whose expenses paid by the government or large tourist enterprises. To get a site included on a familiarisation tour is not easy, but the manager may approach the tourism ministry or perhaps a hotel chain with promotional materials.

If no outside funding is available stakeholders may be able to offer or raise financial support. If foreign press are invited, local business people are more likely to contribute time and resources to the event. Familiarisation visits for the international media are most successful if the journalists invited have special interests that match the activities of a site, such as the theatre or marine protection. One method of identifying appropriate journalists is to find their by-lines in the international press.

PROMOTION OF TOURISM IN PROTECTED AREAS

Tourism activities in and around protected areas can have both positive and negative impacts on local people and the environment. Tourism can benefit a national park or other protected area by serving as a financing mechanism, with direct revenues from user fees and taxes used to protect biological resources and maintain natural areas. Intangible benefits can include increased awareness of and support for the purpose and role of protected areas, by both local communities and tourists. If tourism is important to the local or national economy, it may encourage authorities to manage and maintain protected areas more effectively, benefiting tourists, local communities and the environment. The negative environmental impacts of tourism can include water and soil contamination from construction or improper disposal of solid waste and wastewater, air pollution from transportation, wildlife habitat destruction, and land degradation.

Successfully addressing the challenges of tourism in protected areas requires strong co-operation among all parties, including those operating within and outside protected area boundaries, as well as those that can promote effective management of protected areas by ensuring that the appropriate planning and management tools are adopted. Although the goals of different stakeholders can be quite varied, tourism activities can only be sustainable if implemented with a common understanding and consensus-based approach to development.

Tour operators play a central role in the tourism industry. As intermediaries between tourists and tourism service suppliers, tour operators can influence the choices of consumers, the practices of suppliers and the development patterns of destinations. This unique role means that tour operators can make an important contribution to furthering the goals of sustainable tourism development and protecting the environmental and cultural resources on which the tourism industry depends for its survival and growth. The members of the Tour Operators' Initiative believe that tourism in protected areas should be:

— Developed and implemented with the consensus of, and in close co-operation with, relevant stakeholders;

— Supported by effective policies, guidelines, management strategies and technical tools; and o Focused on conserving the environment while ensuring economically, socially and culturally sound development.

The members of the Tour Operators' Initiative also believe that tour operators can contribute to the sustainable development of tourism in protected areas in many different ways, such as:

— Including protected areas in their itineraries and giving customers information about the natural and cultural features of visited sites and their roles in the conservation of local ecosystems;

— Limiting the size of their groups, or dividing large groups into smaller ones when visiting protected areas;

— Informing protected area managers of visits ahead of time and discussing ways to reduce visitor impacts;

— Integrating sustainability principles into the selection criteria and service agreements of their suppliers, and choosing locally owned and operated suppliers;

— Making financial contributions to conservation and development projects;

—· Providing customers with opportunities to proactively support protected areas; and

— Providing customers with guidelines on how to avoid negative impacts while visiting sensitive areas, for example by maintaining appropriate distances from wildlife, staying on trails to avoid trampling plants or causing erosion, and keeping water and energy use down to avoid related impacts on the environment.

Discovery Initiatives (UK) offers Discoverer Holidays, which allow customers to get involved as field assistants in specific research projects. For example, a tour in Kalimantan, Indonesia, on the island of Borneo, allows travellers to work with the world's leading orang-utan study programme and contributes US$1,000 per client to the Orang-utan Foundation in Tanjing Putung National Park. Dynamic Tours (Morocco) has developed a Mountain and Desert Guide's Charter for its guides, as a means to build awareness on their roles as liaisons to travellers on:

— Environmental problems;

— Economic impacts of groups in a given area;

— Financial resources generated by tourism and their role in preserving local species and heritage;

— Local social and economic development; and

— Appropriate and sustainable environmental and social practices.

Exodus (UK) has a Responsible Tourism policy that includes:

— Hiring more local guides to provide better experiences and support to local communities;

— Purchasing local products and services, where appropriate, for all trips;

— Working with local operators to implement the policy; and

— Limiting group size based on local situations.

Hapag-Lloyd Kreuzfahrten (Germany) specialises in expedition and luxury river and ocean cruises, particularly in the Arctic, Antarctica, the South Pacific Islands and the Amazon basin. To minimise the environmental impacts of its tours and improve the experience of its customers, the company has developed a handbook for travellers to Antarctica, which provides:

— Guidelines and practical information for appropriate behaviour in Antarctica;

— Historical, geological and scientific facts to accompany lectures offered on cruises; and

— Supplementary reading on Antarctica, covering topics such as the region's history, the Antarctic Treaty, native plants and animals, and environmental issues in the region.

Hotelplan (Switzerland) established an Eco-Fund in January 2001. Funds are raised through a contribution of five Swiss Francs (about US$3) per customer on any of Hotelplan's 'Holidays at the Seaside' packages, which represent 20-25 percent of sales. In 2002, the fund raised about US$750,000. The money is used for internal and external sustainable tourism projects, environmental efforts by partners at Hotelplan destinations, and emergency help in case of natural disasters or one-off projects.

Premier Tours (US), which specialises in safari tours to Southern and East Africa, selects tented camps and lodges in national parks and private game reserves that are committed to sustainable practices and apply a sensible approach to tourism, conservation and local community involvement. Premier Tours favours camps that:

— Employ full-time ecologists to ensure sustainable environmental practices in camps;

— Provide electricity through solar panels;

— Do not allow hunting, but support photographic safaris;

— Provide for direct or indirect benefits to local communities and/or conservation projects;

— Have garbage removed to appropriate places for safe disposal; and

— Have lined tanks for safe sewage processing.

TUI Nederland (the Netherlands) launched the Environmentally Aware Tourism project in Bonaire and Curaçao in 1999, to provide customers with information on responsible travel and sustainable products. Initial information is provided in the brochures of TUI Nederland's brands Arke and Holland International. Once a client has chosen a holiday to Bonaire or Curaçao:

— TUI Nederland provides tips for environmentally sound practices in the voucher booklet that includes their air tickets;

— KLM, a project partner, shows an on-board video about the sustainable excursions and activities that are part of the project;

— Upon arrival, trained TUI Nederland hostesses introduce guests to the sustainable excursions and activities that are available; and

— The TUI Nederland resource book, available in hotel lobbies, further directs guests to sustainable excursions, activities and attractions.

Viaggi del Ventaglio (Italy) decided in 1998 to grant US$1 per bed/night to the Ministry of Tourism of the Dominican Republic, to help repair damage from Hurricane George. Contributions lasted for one year and generated about US$150,000. Part of the funds were invested in the conservation and development of Saona Island, inside the Parque Nacional del Este.

The island represents a unique and beautiful, but delicate, ecosystem, and is a favourite excursion for hotels located in the area. Funds were also used to reconstruct 63 houses in the village of Manojuan, which was badly damaged by the hurricane, and to promote and develop local handicrafts, through grants to local enterprises.

DESTINATION PROMOTION : TOUR OPERATORS' ROLE

Tour operators is the most important factor in the tourism industry. As intermediaries between tourists and tourism service suppliers, tour operators can make an important contribution to furthering the goals of sustainable tourism development and protecting the environmental and cultural resources on which the tourism industry depends for its survival and growth. It is thus in the tour operators' interest to preserve the environment in destinations and establish good relationships with local communities, to improve the quality of their tourism products and increase customer satisfaction. The members of the Tour Operators' Initiative for Sustainable Tourism Development (TOI) recognise that they cannot achieve their sustainability goals without working in partnership with all stakeholders in the destinations where they operate.

TOI Partnerships

TOI members have committed to establish and strengthen links and develop partnerships with local authorities, the private sector, civil society and non-governmental organisations (NGOs) in the destinations they visit. The TOI's network offers its members the opportunity to approach them together, with a common voice, and develop in a full participatory approach a shared vision on sustainable development and a common action plan, which is the base for a solid partnership between tour operators and the various destination stakeholders.

Side, on the southern coast of Turkey, is the first destination in which the TOI members have forged a partnership with the local stakeholders. TOI members and their local partners bring to Side approximately 300,000 tourists each year. To prepare the grounds for the partnership, local stakeholders and TOI members were interviewed on their individual views of the key sustainability threats in Side. These interviews were then followed by a multi-stakeholder Workshop in April 2002, organised with the support of one of the TOI members, VASCO Travel, and TUDER, the local hotel association. The meeting was attended by the Mayor of Side, representatives of WWF Turkey, and representatives of the private sector, including the Manavgat Chamber of Commerce (MATSO), individual hoteliers, excursion providers and local travel agencies. Several TOI members, along with representatives of UNEP, UNESCO and WTO/OMT, were also present.

The meeting gave the participants the opportunity to share their views on the main threats to sustainability in the Side region and ways to address these. The participants agreed on three priority actions:

— Waste management (with a focus on waste separation and recycling).

— Education and training on sustainable tourism in hotels, bars and restaurants.

— Promotion of Side's culture and cultural activities.

The participants also agreed on the benefit of a continuous dialogue between tour operators and local stakeholders. During follow up meetings with local stakeholders, a detailed plan of action was developed, and a locally based coordinator was appointed, financed by the Side administration and TUDER. Activities implemented in the two years include:

— A waste separation scheme has been designed and is now in operation in the municipality of Side. Recycling companies have been identified and pick-up times for participating hotels have been set.

— The local recycling company posts signs on its vehicles to promote the Side initiative, and hotels and restaurants post signs at their entrances.

— The Side Tourism Association (TUDER) has placed containers for collecting used batteries in every Side hotel, in the Ali Ihsan Barut elementary school and in the Tourism Hotel Vocational High School.

— Waste separation bins for organic and recyclable waste have been placed in Side for use by residents and tourists.

— Training sessions on solid waste management and waste separation techniques, organised with technical input and background material from UNEP, were held for managers and staff at hotels, apartment hotels and pensions; Side Municipality sanitation workers; sanitation manager and association presidents; members of the Garment Association and of the Bar and Restaurant Association.

Today, over 100 hotels and all local shops and restaurants participate in the waste separation scheme. Data from the last seven months of 2003 are promising: 276 tons of inorganic waste, and 11.978 batteries were collected. Moreover, the new land fill area has been identified and approved and it will be in operations in Summer 2004.

A second TOI partnership has been initiated with Bayahibe, PuntaCana and Bavaro, three of the most visited destinations in the Dominican Republic. Following informal discussions and visits, a Sustainable Tourism Round Table was convened in December 2003, in collaboration with the Bayahibe-La Romana Hotel Association and the Punta Cana Group. The Round Table was also made possible thanks to the financial and technical contribution of the German Technical Cooperation (GTZ), and Conservation International's Center for Environmental Leadership in Business. The participants of the Round Table committed to an Agenda for Action, that include:

— Establishment of a 'Garbage free' zone,

— Improved management of the marine excursions to Isla Saona in Parque del Este,

— Process for greater community involvement,

— Support by tour operators of a promotional program for the hoteliers in Bayahibe that implement social and environmental programs.

Participants agreed also on the creation of a Co-ordinating Body that include the Bayahibe-La Romana Hotel Association, the Del Este Hotels Association, the associations of Excursion and local tour operators, the Punta Cana Ecological Foundation, the Bavaro Reef Fund, Ecoparques, the office of the Archbishop of La Altagracia, and the Tour Operators' Initiative. The Co-ordinating Body will oversee the implementation of the agenda and support the continuous communication and co-ordination of actions among all players.

People's Practicipation in Destination Promotion

Unravelling the identity and structure of different stakeholder groups can be time consuming and the results are not obvious. For example, different agencies can be involved in the management of a site and have different goals and objectives. In many cases, several agencies control various sections of a protected World Heritage site, each with its own management strategy. While sharing a common heritage resource, visitor management strategies and issues vary from one area to the next. Some stakeholders are unwilling to support wider participation, especially when it is seen as a threat to their authority. For example, managers may accept a policy of openness and communication but may resist supplying all pertinent information to interest groups. This situation eventually creates a climate of distrust, limiting the site manager's ability to deal with the public.

The most vocal critics can dominate the participation process. Many citizens view public participation as a means of influencing policies and decisions. Public hearings can become forums in which the most vocal critics of a plan can dominate discussions and exclude others from the process. This can happen if an organised lobby group is heavily represented. Some people with legitimate concerns may be intimidated by a venue such as a meeting hall and be afraid to speak up. Alternative venues such as community centres can facilitate a more comfortable exchange of ideas and encourage balanced communication among stakeholders.

Large numbers of people may be overlooked because they are not as vocal as other groups. Any issue that generates public interest is subject to a wide range of opinion. While most people will have an opinion, many will not feel strongly about the issue. This large majority risks being ignored. It may be felt that they are the group that can be most influenced because they are not very interested and are probably not well informed. The possibility of some event igniting the interest of this less-interested majority should however not be underestimated. Consideration of these groups is essential to ensuring long-term public support.

Hierarchical structures may inhibit stakeholder participation in decision making. In many societies the formal structure of institutions and organisations as well as cultural norms may make it difficult to elicit the opinions of certain groups making stakeholder participation in formal meetings impossible. A few powerful agencies may dominate, overwhelming other stakeholders and blocking cooperation. In some countries, the government is directly involved in the actual business of tourism, functioning as tour operators as well as making policy, which may lead to imbalances in stakeholder input.

Public participation may be more a form of appeasement than a way to solicit stakeholders' input. Offering local communities the opportunity to participate raises expectations about acceptance of their suggestions. A government may try to guide a particular choice either by representing only one opinion or by proposing a set of choices among which only one is tenable. Decisions may have already been made before public participation begins; any changes may be minor with relatively small impacts. Before embarking on a participatory planning exercise, proponents have to be ready to change original plans according to the input received.

Overemphasis on involving stakeholder groups can lead to a failure to recognise certain effects on resources. Managers must understand how stakeholders perceive impacts and define acceptability. However, many stakeholder groups have limited knowledge about natural and cultural resources and may be unaware of potential negative impacts. Visitors adapt to deteriorating environmental conditions, accepting degradation as the inevitable result of increasing visitation. The visitors who are displeased by the degradation may not return and are not captured by surveys and public involvement efforts.

Other stakeholder groups may be concerned only with economic considerations that could outweigh the desire to protect resources. So, while public participation is necessary, over-reliance on public input can lead to inaction and a deterioration of conditions over time. With resource bases declining and the demand for recreation and tourist attractions on the rise, it is managers who must ultimately decide the parameters of how much and what kinds of tourism activity are acceptable.

Trust is the crucial element of successful public participation. Building trust and a willingness to participate depends on several factors. Positive earlier interaction builds trust. The history of the experiences with, for example, a state government agency influences the chances of fostering participation. Rebuilding relations between conservation authorities and local people after a history of policing and exclusion can be difficult. H.S. Panwar, who taught at the Wildlife Institute of India at Dehra Dun, reported that the main criteria of success in ecologically oriented development projects were building trust and enrolling the full participation of local people in the planning and implementation process.

Honouring commitments builds trust. Amboseli National Park in Kenya, La Amistad National Park in Costa Rica and Panama, and Yellowstone National Park in the United States have all had problems with local communities after funding cuts that forced policy changes. At Amboseli, a lack of funding for maintaining pumps at watering facilities caused a gap in trust with park officials and impinged on the needs of local Maasai cattle herders.

At La Amistad and Yellowstone, personnel and budget cuts took a financial toll on the local communities. Gestures that show equality, for example, sharing information equally among stakeholders, promote trust. From its inception, the Great Barrier Reef project worked from a scientific information base, regularly issuing maps, data and carefully prepared information to the public.

Time is necessary to build trust. Many experts agree that more time and effort could be spent addressing the various agendas of interest groups. One researcher writes, "Trust-building takes time. The history of rural development initiatives is littered with enough examples to indicate that such time is a resource well spent in terms of effective policy outcomes." A non-partisan image helps build trust with stakeholders. When a particular problem arises at a site, the site manager — who is seen as a government official-may be wise to ask a popular local personality to explain the matter to the public.

If time and money permit, credible scientific information can serve as non-partisan evidence to heighten public understanding of an issue and change people's minds. Yellowstone officials published pertinent scientific information, viewed as more neutral, in the daily newspaper to advise the public about a project to reintroduce wolves into the park.

A process calling for participation and collaboration has been found to be more conducive to consensus than traditional methods involving expert planners only. Work in community extension projects has shown more progress in community relations when participatory methods are used. Experts report that no point is too early in the project cycle to begin inviting local participation. A participatory approach is beneficial in several ways:

— While issues of power and control will not disappear certain individuals will always be motivated to convert others to their position the participatory process enhances communication by showing both the common ground and the differences between the stakeholder groups. The exercise often leads to compromise and a breakdown of defensive positions.

— Evidence suggests that people are reluctant to divulge past difficulties. Informal communication systems such as surveys can help get people to reveal their interests and concerns. Reports from the North Pennines Tourism Partnership programme in England revealed that such informal communication helped to resolve issues between the different groups.

— Public involvement tends to build momentum towards collaborative implementation. As one researcher has pointed out, misunderstandings between groups, rather than a lack of information, is at the core of many social difficulties.

Communication Techniques

Participatory techniques such as rural appraisals allow local people to describe their environment. Participatory Rural Appraisals (PRAs) can facilitate the exchange of informal information between local government officials, NGO staff and local people. These methods have proven capable of overcoming the problems of listening and shaping an accurate assessment of stakeholder concerns. The techniques help map out local resources, ways people make a living, trends in resource use, and the local costs and benefits of conservation and protection. They are practical methods of encouraging local participation, fostering communication and making a more accurate appraisal of local concerns. The utility of these methods has been demonstrated in many areas of the world, particularly in Pakistan and India. Participatory techniques, including PRAs, can be used for both natural and cultural sites.

Alternative forms of dialogue can help limit public confrontations. Public meetings can be ineffective when the parties with the most vested interests attend with the goal of pressing their particular causes. Less confrontational meeting structures can reduce such undue influence and limit the posturing of interest groups for the press. During the controversial Yellowstone wolf reintroduction project, open houses were held where individual people could sit down in a relaxed atmosphere and talk directly with representatives of the various agencies involved. Special meetings were held to allow powerful interest groups to voice their opinions, but they were listening sessions only. These were run by female park officials, perceived as less threatening and non-partisan than male officials, and local police were hired to maintain order.

The process of developing a management plan can encourage the participation of stakeholders. The process can also be used to build consensus. However, instead of releasing draft management plans for public comment, planners should begin by identifying what is needed from the public, and what a site can offer them in return. Plans and strategies should be developed slowly, be dynamic and adaptable, and be concise rather than lengthy. Above all, they should be inclusive of all stakeholders. Examples of successful issue-based management planning include the great Smokey Mountains National Park in the United States, where many trails were in poor condition and needed to be closed to have time to recover. Park managers realised that closing trails would generate negative sentiment. To educate the public about the situation, management decided to involve people in the process. Meetings were held to give people an understanding of the park's mission and to provide them with an opportunity to participate in setting priorities. At the Willandra Lakes Region World Heritage site, in Australia, a five-day workshop was held at which community members helped write the first draft of a management plan. The exercise guaranteed continued support for the plan. At the Shark Bay World Heritage site, also in Australia, participatory management plans for conservation areas are also made available for public comment for at least two months, a practice required under Western Australian law.

An advisory group or stakeholders' organisation can play a crucial role in the success of management objectives. Consultation with various interest groups through regular meetings and public workshops offers opportunities for stakeholders to comment on a preliminary management plan. This relationship enables site managers to bring local people into decision-making. Ongoing conflicts will not necessarily go away, but an advisory group provides a structure for the problem-solving process so that conflicts and solutions can be identified more clearly.

Public participation is more likely to be effective and sustained through stakeholder groups than through individual participation. At the Shark Bay World Heritage site, an advisory committee played a major role in determining appropriate and practical strategies for management of the reserves and the region's resources, including setting the boundaries of the site. As was previously mentioned, Patan, a town in the Kathmandu Valley, Nepal, has a citizens' advisory group developing a tourism programme to aid preservation of the community's historic buildings. At Tangariro National Park in New Zealand, a Maori burial site became a popular rock-climbing area. Because this use of the site was of great concern to the Maori, meetings were held between the climbers and tribal elders with the result that the climbers agreed to practise voluntary restraint in using the area.

Non-governmental organisations (NGOs) can play an important role in linking tourism stakeholders. NGOs can act as intermediaries between the private sector and local interests. In some countries NGOs with computers and communications equipment can serve as links between stakeholders without such resources. There is reason to believe that NGOs' prestige can bring added pressure to bear in negotiations with private tourism companies.

CHAPTER 4

TOURISM MARKET OPERATIONS

The tourism market comprises three general classi-
fications:

1. the independent travel market,
2. the speciality activity market, and
3. the general package-holiday market.

Independent travellers are not part of organised groups but
travel alone or in small groups of friends. They travel
either out of a general interest or because they want to
practise a certain activity in a new and different
environment. Most independent travellers are young,
adventurous, willing to use rustic accommodations, eat
traditional foods, and take public transport. Independent
travellers get much of their information on a tourist
destination either from friends who have visited the area
or through guidebooks, newspaper and magazine articles,
or, increasingly, from the Internet. Many in the tourism
industry discount these tourists because they tend to
travel cheaply, falling into the category of the budget-
conscious "backpacking crowd". In reality, independent
travellers are "explorers" who are often responsible for
popularising a destination. Their financial input is often
enough to enable local businesses to expand and improve
rustic accommodations for more demanding tourist
groups. Such travellers, often young, are more willing to
use local goods and services, and interact more with the

community outside the supervision of an organised tour, which unfortunately may cause negative social impacts.

Speciality tourism firms organise trips for clients wishing to participate in a specific activity such as bird-watching, wildlife viewing, photography or archaeological, historical and cultural tours. Also in this category are adventure travel firms offering activities such as backpacking/ trekking, white water rafting, kayaking, canoeing, rock climbing and sport fishing. Other speciality firms organise field research trips for scientists. These firms attract groups of paying volunteers who sign up to work as field assistants on projects such as archaeological digs and wildlife monitoring programmes. In addition, this market includes organisations and universities with special interest travel programmes. For example, the World-wide Fund for Nature and many museums organise tours for their members. These tours generally help to raise funds for a particular cause or project. These groups generally sub-contract to other tour operators to handle the travel arrangements. Speciality tour operators commonly use host-country ground operators for in-country logistics. These national firms, based in the country in which the tour is operating, provide all services from arrival to departure. Some speciality firms in North America and Europe handle ground operations in a foreign country for themselves, but they tend to be exceptions to the rule. Managers should be aware that many speciality companies are small and go in and out of business rapidly.

The general package-holiday market attracts groups wishing to see an area and its culture but without a specific interest in a defined activity or subject matter. These tourists tend to be interested in general sightseeing and shopping, and may be interested in cultural attractions such as museums, ruins or other well-known or documented historical sites. Tourists in this market tend to want the standard services and amenities offered by most general tours. They will probably not be satisfied with the services that a rural community can offer; more often than not, general international tour groups want comfort, ease of access, security and more upscale accommodations and food.

SPECIALITY ACTIVITY MARKETS

Markets or market segments have been developed around the different activities. Specialised holidays have become so popular that whole new categories of travel have emerged, including ecotourism, adventure travel, heritage tourism and cultural tourism. A trek in the Himalayas is now likely to be considered adventure travel, and a week visiting cultural sites in India as cultural tourism.

Eco-tourism

Eco-tourism is one of the most frequently cited categories of the "new" tourism. It is the responsible travel to natural areas that conserves the environment and sustains the well being of local people. A number of activities have been labelled eco-tourism, including bird- and whale-watching, helping scientists conduct conservation research, snorkelling off coral reefs, game viewing and nature photography. Eco-tourism is linked to and overlaps with heritage tourism and cultural tourism. Surveys show that eco-tourists tend to be young and highly educated, with professional and managerial occupations.

Eco-tourism trips tend to be longer, with fewer people in the typical tour group. Researchers report that eco-tourists are more likely to use small independent hotels, as opposed to mass tourists, who tend to stay at chain hotels. As would be expected, the eco-tourist is interested in a more natural environment, preferring less crowded destinations that are off the beaten track and that offer challenging experiences. At the site level, the demands of eco-tourists and mainstream tourists may overlap and be difficult to differentiate. Some eco-tourists, for example, may demand condominiums, not campgrounds, for lodging. People on a bird-watching cruise to Patagonia could be considered eco-tourists but may have demands similar to those of tourists on an expensive Caribbean islands cruise. In practice, eco-tourism connotes a travel ethic, promoting conservation behaviours and certain economic policies. Examples are, an emphasis on low-impact techniques for viewing wildlife and a preference for hiring local guides.

Adventure Tourism

Adventure tourism includes a wide range of outdoor activities: Adventure tourists engage in activities that are physically challenging and sometimes dangerous, or perceived to be so. Examples are sports such as trekking, mountaineering, white-water rafting and scuba diving. Adventure tourism does not necessarily require expensive facilities and infrastructure, but it does require good organisation, guides, transportation services, basic accommodation in the field, and opportunities for more comfortable accommodation at the end of the tour. Adventure travel is a rapidly growing sector of the speciality tourism market.

Cultural Tourism

Cultural tourism is frequently used to describe certain segments of the travel market: It may be associated with visits to historical, artistic and scientific or heritage attractions. The World Tourism Organisation (WTO) has two definitions of cultural tourism. In the narrow sense, cultural tourism includes "movements of persons for essentially cultural motivations such as study tours, performing arts and cultural tours, travel to festivals and other cultural events, visits to sites and monuments, travel to study nature, folklore or art, and pilgrimages." In the broader sense it is defined as "all movements of persons, because they satisfy the human need for diversity, tending to raise the cultural level of the individual and giving rise to new knowledge, experience and encounters."

Heritage Tourism

Heritage tourism is a broad category that embraces both eco-tourism and cultural tourism, with an emphasis on conserving natural and cultural heritage: It is a category or market segment that includes visits to historic sites, museums and art galleries, and exploring national and forest parks. Heritage tourism, because of the large number of activities it covers, is difficult to define and measure. In recent years city planners interested in urban regeneration have adopted the term to describe many tourism programmes, a strategy that has received support from business and banks. Many other tourism terms reflect environmental ethics and local interests. Environmental preservation concerns have given rise to what is known as green tourism, conservation-supporting tourism, and environmentally aware or environmentally sound tourism. Generally, such tourism favours minimal environmental impact and emphasises concern over environmental issues. Urban and rural tourism categories have also been created. However, since few countries have made the distinction, quantification has been difficult.

Sustainable Tourism

The idea of sustainability is found in all the market segments and definitions of the "new" tourism. All the definitions address preservation of the resource for future generations; the use of tourism to contribute to environmental protection; limiting negative socio-economic impacts, and benefiting local people economically and socially. The WTO defines sustainable tourism as: "Tourism development that meets the needs of the present tourists and host regions while protecting and enhancing opportunity for the future. The desired outcome is that resources will be managed in such a way that economic, social and aesthetic needs can be fulfilled while maintaining cultural integrity, essential ecological processes, biological diversity and life support systems."

The term "sustainable tourism" is frequently used in project proposals seeking international assistance. In practice, sustainable tourism programmes are an opportunity that also demands hard work. They require clearly defined goals and objectives that highlight the essential features of sustainability within the local context, an ongoing process of addressing stakeholder needs within the framework of these goals and objectives, and constant monitoring. As with all sustainable development projects, this process is labour intensive, takes time and usually involves many interest groups, making programmes difficult to design, implement and maintain. Sustainable tourism programmes have highlighted the need for an environmental and social focus and led to the standardisation of some environmental practices as well as new ideas about how the industry should function. Discussion has produced policy goals and guidelines for planners and an impetus for self-regulation by the industry.

TRENDS IN TOURISM MARKETS

More and more consumers want a high standard of environmental conservation coupled with simple, efficient and pleasant service. It appears that many tourists now prefer unspoiled and uncrowded destinations. A related trend is that, before they travel, many tourists inform themselves about environmental problems at individual sites. They want destinations to be clean and environmentally sound. Tourists will avoid places that are perceived to fall short of this image. More than ever this information is obtained through the internet. Environmental degradation can lead not only to declining tourism rates but also to changes in the types of tourists that travel to a site. Examples of this cycle are found in the Mediterranean, where the pattern has led to continued degradation and urbanisation of beach resorts.

Interest in cultural tourism seems to be expanding, but the rate of growth is unclear. More quantitative data is needed to verify the trend. For example, attendance at cultural attractions in Britain and the Netherlands over the last five years indicates that cultural tourism has kept pace with the overall tourism market. Because the cultural tourism market is difficult to quantify, experts suggest that more research would help to identify broad groupings of cultural tourists based on their motivations. Establishing categories such as arts, archaeology, language learning and so on may be the most practical way to address this issue.

Tourists increasingly want "real" experiences with other cultures and lifestyles. A study of massmarket tourists and eco-tourists found that both groups felt that knowledge of folk arts and handicrafts, as well as knowledge about the destination's history, was important. Consumers are seeking more active and educational holidays. Specialised markets are experiencing a trend towards energetic, environment-oriented tourism, with healthy menus and plenty of opportunities for exercise. Although mass-market tourists are less active and adventuresome, and less focused on one activity, active holidays at a lower level of intensity are also a growing trend in this market segment.

Visits to protected areas are on the rise. In developed countries, tourists tend to travel in smaller groups for shorter time periods. For example, visits to Australian national parks have increased substantially in the last ten years, but often for shorter periods. The two trends together-smaller group sizes and shorter stays- have created a need for greater individual space and more facilities designed to accommodate intense use, with extra services added during certain times of the year.

The tourism industry is expected to take more responsibility for sustainable development. Professionals working in conservation are beginning to ask the industry to be more involved in site management activities. Often this involves assuming a degree of financial responsibility for the long-term maintenance of the resources they profit from. Financial support can be in the form of direct or voluntary subsidies to management agencies or NGOs. Involvement may also mean accepting practices that limit the negative impacts of tourism.

Operators are prohibited from relocating their facilities and activities once an existing site is affected by natural or unnatural environmental degradation has reinforced these actions.

— Tourism definitions can give direction to broad policy guidelines used in the development of goals and objectives for site management. For example, the International Eco-tourism Society's definition of eco-tourism states that tourism should maintain the integrity of an ecosystem and generate economic opportunities that make conservation beneficial to local people. This type of a statement can be incorporated into a policy statement defining the type of tourism a site will promote.

— Tourism definitions, such as that of eco-tourism, can be used in reports or proposals seeking funding for future projects. They can give documents a positive image and strengthen their attractiveness. Overall development concepts and definitions should match the audience for whom the proposal is being written. For example, the term eco-tourism should be used in place of tourism when writing to nature conservation organisations; cultural tourism when writing to organisations concerned with the restoration of monuments, and so on. Market definitions can then be used in promotional materials. For example, a brochure may mention that eco-tourism is encouraged at a particular natural or mixed site.

— Operators' promotional materials give clues as to whether their products are compatible with site objectives. Tour operator literature can also help managers determine whether operators contribute locally to protec-tion efforts such as educating clients in low-impact practices. Promotional literature will also reveal the types of clients they are targeting, what kind of experiences they value and their particular needs. For example, an operator may specialise in tours geared to a serious, single-minded bird-watching group or an amateur archaeology group.

— While knowledge of tourism definitions and speciality tourist markets can help managers set policy guidelines and understand visitor interests, the categories are general and tend to overlap. For management purposes it is useful to classify and analyse tourists according to their preferences and behaviours. Categories such as "hard" and "soft" class provide a helpful start. These categories, which focus on visitor needs and expectations, are important for elaborating management plans and setting objectives including infrastructure development.

— Knowledge of the different market segments and the general behaviours and preferences of tourists can help managers decide which segments to promote. Different tourists present different management opportunities and requirements. For example, tourists seeking more demanding or "harder" experiences are more likely to be content with a minimal infrastructure than those seeking a "softer" experience. Tour operators such as those working with keen bird-watchers or clients interested in archaeology may have special market demands. These specialised operators may want strict regulation of tourist numbers and noise to permit them to practise their activities undisturbed by other groups. In view of the range of preferences among nature-oriented people, the market should offer a range of accommodation.

— An analysis of the structure of the tourism industry surrounding a site can reveal opportunities for involving stakeholders in management. NTO officials could be involved in future promotional efforts. Tour operators and hoteliers who may also help with monitoring activities or establishing codes of conduct and minimal impact practices. They may also make direct financial contributions for on-site projects. Interviews with tour operators and hotel directors could determine what mechanisms, administrative and financial, would facilitate their contributions to conservation and protection efforts.

— A proactive approach will yield benefits if market trends are addressed. Continued growth in international tourism is predicted, particularly in special interest tourism. The growing concern over environmental and socio-cultural issues suggests the existence of a large potential source of support for the site. Socio-economic profiles suggest that more and more tourists will have the means to contribute financially towards protection of the site.

Consequently, if a site is planned and managed well, within defined limits, an increase in arrivals can potentially bring new financial rewards.

— Because tourists are more conscious of, and interested in, the protection of the natural, historical, cultural and social environment, it will be increasingly important to inform tourists and tour operators, through site interpretation and promotional activities, of the efforts that management is making to maintain the site.

— A preference for protected areas is a growing trend in tourism. Managers must be increasingly cognizant of these visitors' profiles and of visitation trends specific to each site.

SETTING POLICY GOALS

A tourism marketing process may fail to focus on a site's true cultural traditions or historical interpretation and instead package it using an imagined sense of character. World Heritage cultural sites, many incapable of accommodating large volumes of tourists, may use inappropriate modern materials and styles when trying to increase capacity. For example, the Archaeological Survey of India ruled out lighting the grounds of the Taj Mahal. Lights would have made it easier for evening visitors but would have taken away from the experience of seeing the monument by moonlight. A historic town in the United States was practically deserted, raising the question of whether to let the cultural resource continue its natural decline or intervene to restore the site for more intensive tourism. Unfortunately, no old photographs remained from the town's heyday, and experts feared a misrepresentation of the past if restoration was carried out. The state historical society recommended managing the site to permit the town's natural deterioration. Major restorations were rejected in favour of simple shoring and bracing. To accommodate tourism needs, minimal construction activities were recommended including parking, footpaths and signage.

The local historical society, however, recommended that the town be completely restored. It favoured more intensive tourism and was not concerned with philosophical issues and the consequences of intervention. In the end, the town was restored but with doubts remaining over whether the quality, character and authenticity of the site was compromised. Practically, policy decisions are often heavily influenced by economic considerations. A decision on maintaining the values of ancient ruins in relation to the extent to which stabilisation and conservation is carried out may be a function of the funds and personnel available. Allowing visitors to view a ruin from a distance may be more practical and preferable than the more expensive option of structurally stabilising the site to permit visitor access. In some cases all that may be needed is vegetation control to reduce deterioration.

When developing tourism policies at World Heritage sites, the overriding priority is to maintain the form and fabric of the resource. The nomination dossier of a World Heritage site can give guidance to the process of balancing policy and management objectives against tourism needs. These dossiers usually describe a site's features and previous changes in detail and may set out necessary preservation actions. Dossiers are available through each country's State Party and/or through the World Heritage Centre.

Policy goals are broad statements that set out a vision of how a site will be managed on the basis of its environmental and social conditions. Policies guide a variety of actions including building infrastructure and developing social programmes such as promoting local educational and economic development through tourism.

Where this policy development process is a joint exercise, a policy statement can unite people with different viewpoints and give direction to public and private tourism management. The general nature of policy goals is reflected in a policy statement from the Australia Wet Tropics Management Authority. It says the Authority's purpose is to "provide for the implementation of Australia's international duty for the protection, conservation, presentation, rehabilitation and transmission to future generations of the Wet Tropics of Queensland World Heritage Area, within the meaning of the World Heritage Convention."

While policy goals are general, management objectives set out in detail how a site will be managed. Within the framework of the general policy goals, the objectives spell out desired conditions, reflecting what management wants to maintain and the experiences a visitor would ideally encounter at a site. For example, if a policy goal is to provide local employment opportunities, then a management objective may be to encourage the use of local guides. If a goal is to maintain a sacred site in a manner ensuring respect and tranquillity, then objectives may include limiting visitation and noise levels. Objectives should be subject to evaluation. They should therefore be specific, quantifiable, have time limits and be stated in clear language so that they can be understood by all those responsible for implementation. They should be the basis for a standard by which to gauge the performance of site management. For example, at a historical monument, a policy goal may be to support local educational activities, while a management objective could be to increase the number of local schoolchildren who attend the site's educational programme. In this case a quantifiable measure could be the number of school groups that visit the site during the year. Clearly stated policy goals and objectives provide direction in decision making and responding to change. Constructing a tramway through a wilderness park, building a high-rise modern hotel near a low-lying archaeological site, installing artificial lights at a monument, and increasing helicopter traffic in a national park are all examples of tourism initiatives that World Heritage site managers have had to face.

Clearly documented goals and objectives give direction and provide a historical context for addressing tourism initiatives in a consistent manner. Any new initiative can change a site. Examining initiatives within the context of policies and objectives can help managers determine whether they are within acceptable parameters. If goals and objectives are based on stakeholder needs, and fall within the law and the World Heritage Convention, they can form a solid basis for management decision making.

In addition, activities such as interpretation, promotion, carrying capacity control and monitoring all depend on the direction given by policy goals and objectives. A project in the Carpathian Mountains in Eastern Europe illustrates the need for clearly defined tourism policy goals. An international funding agency assigned a team of experts to write a regional tourism development plan to aid small businesses. Market research suggested a comparative advantage for small-scale accommodations, emphasising natural and cultural attractions.

Some members of the government and business community, however, favoured the rebuilding of large-scale tourism infrastructure from the Soviet era. At the time, no unified national or regional policies for tourism development existed to give direction to and clarify these efforts. The disparity of goals persisted throughout the life of the project.

When the time came to present a final report, the team found it impossible to present strategy and cost recommendations that met the needs of both groups. A forest reserve in Costa Rica whose operational budget is largely based on visitor fees had no clear-cut policies on tourism development until several years ago. A project to build a larger visitor centre met with opposition from some in the administration because they saw the site more as a nature reserve than as a tourist destination.

Others liked the idea and wanted to attract more tourists. While members of the community were against it, people in other nearby communities were in favour of increasing tourism because of the economic benefits it would bring. After months of controversy, the issue was resolved with a consultant's study and dialogue among the different stakeholder groups. With an established process within the reserve's administration to discuss policies and define goals, these conflicts would have been minimised and no doubt resolved without outside help.

Stakeholders' Involvement in Setting Goals

Stakeholder concerns should make up the list of management issues from which policy goals and objectives are developed: Stakeholders' involvement in setting goals and objectives links a tourism strategy with those who will have an impact on a site now and in the future. Stakeholders can be consulted on a number of management concerns such as infrastructure development and monitoring programmes. Stakeholders usually include government officials, members of the environmental and conservation community, scientists, historic preservation organisations, hotel and tour agency owners, visitors, guides and residents. Following is a list of stakeholders with suggestions on how they may contribute to developing tourism goals and objectives.

— Park, forestry or archaeological department officials may provide information on past management and visitor issues.

— Guides can offer information on the social and environmental conditions of the site, and their input can bring to light important interpretation issues.

— Guides working for tourist agencies can give advice on their employers' concerns and input on site monitoring needs.

— Community leaders often have concerns and ideas about how tourism will affect local social values and economic development. For example, local leaders may think it necessary to avoid tourism impacts on the main population centre.

— Hotel owners can have a direct influence on tourism development and community interactions. They may be concerned about potential crowding, or coordinating visitor arrivals between the hotel and site management personnel through a reservation system. Hotel owners can also help in the development of interpretation and promotional materials.

— Tour operators will have concerns about visitor comfort and security. They stay apprised of changes in the international travel market and usually have information on user preferences and demand. The value of contacting tour operators to discuss their concerns, potential demand for a site, and possible cooperation on activities such as marketing should not be underestimated.

— Scientists can spell out concerns about significant flora and fauna or historical or archaeological remains. They can suggest ways to protect resources from impacts and offer advice on attracting research grants. Field assistants working directly with scientists can share practical concerns and complementary information.

When developing goals and objectives, libraries and department archives are useful sources of valuable supplemental information, for example on endemic or endangered species of fauna or flora, or on visitor use and impacts on wildlife or archaeological ruins. National tourism and protected area laws and policies including the legal requirements for licensing and taxation can help in setting government policies and in understanding current conditions of tourism development.

Problems faced by Stakeholders

Conflicts with the local community may prevent cooperation in tourism development. For this reason consultation with community members during planning is essential. They may voice concerns that development will bring increased pollution or crime; that tourist traffic may endanger their children; or that tourists will have a negative impact on social conditions, for example by wearing inappropriate dress. They also may fear that the development will not benefit local people, for example that jobs as guides will be given to outsiders. Consultations may result in actions such as the creation of a tourism development committee or a system for training local guides. Tour operators may be asked to educate their clients to respect community values. A visitor centre may be built some distance away from the village to avoid encroaching on everyday village life.

Environmentalists and conservationists have important concerns over the potential negative impacts of tourism development on natural and cultural sites: Environmentalists involved in the protection of flora and fauna may fear that opening an area for tourism could also invite hunters, or they may voice concern over potential disturbances to nesting birds, for example. Archaeologists might warn against vandalism and other potential damage to ruins and monuments. Both groups may complain about increased litter, particularly if existing funds are insufficient for garbage collection. Both are likely to press for conditions in which visitors do not feel rushed or crowded, or spend too much time waiting to enter a site. Members of this stakeholder group often complain of a lack of communication with the tourism sector, including both the ministry and private operators. They may also complain that staff members value tourism development more than educational activities and scientific research. This stakeholder group might wish to persuade site managers to implement an efficient reservation system, to limit access to areas with pristine, fragile ecosystems or to vulnerable archaeological sites, and to mount an education campaign to minimise impacts. They might insist on strict supervision of visitors, especially student science groups. Researchers often advocate the appointment of a science adviser at the site who could promote and manage research. Agreement could be reached on specific targets for tourism promotion and development.

Tour guides are a valuable source of information and advice concerning conditions affecting the environment as well as the visitor experience. They will point out unsafe trail sections and help ensure that trails are maintained for comfortable walking, as well as alert management to problems of crowding and noise. Guides can inform management when local people use the site for hunting and killing birds and other wildlife. Like the environmentalists and conservationists, guides are usually concerned about the quality of their clients' experience, and will insist that the time it takes to purchase a ticket be kept to a minimum, that congestion on the access road to the site be eliminated, and so on. They may suggest maintaining limits on the numbers of visitors permitted at a site through use of an effective reservation system, and measures such as staggering visits by promoting afternoon tours. A direct telephone or radio connection between site management staff and guides would ensure consistent and effective communication.

Hotel owners and managers usually want a site to provide a broad base of opportunities for different types of visitors. They are also concerned about crowding and littering, the amount of parking at the site entrance, and the presence of persistent beggars and/or souvenir hawkers. As with independent guides, hotels appreciate consistent and reliable communication with site management, perhaps by a specially installed direct phone line. Members of this stakeholder group might ask staff management to develop a reservation system for tours. They would also advocate formation of a tourism advisory committee to meet with the local community about development issues and the needs and preferences of tourists.

Overseas tour operators and ground operators are especially concerned about logistical questions. Will their tour groups have to wait in line behind other tours scheduled at the same time? Will their groups meet up with noisy or inconsiderate groups? Is there enough parking? And, as with other shareholder groups, operators are anxious for a site to be well maintained and safe for visitors, and in the case of natural sites that the wildlife are adequately protected. These stakeholders often advocate efficient reservation systems, good communications and regular maintenance.

A stakeholder advisory group can facilitate the development of policy goals and management objectives: Such a panel provides a mechanism for exchanging ideas and information. The group should draft a written policy or vision statement that can be developed and publicly endorsed. The group could also help to set management objectives, including standards for desired conditions and actions. Practically, stakeholder groups can be engaged in the management process and serve as forums for exchanging views and reaching agreement on tourism issues. If an advisory group is not feasible, some mechanism for exchanging ideas is needed. This can be as simple as a regular exchange of memos between site management staff and stakeholder groups, to solicit opinions and describe current activities. The process of developing goals and objectives should also take into account the site's uniqueness in relation to other sites with which it competes. Tour operators and other tourism professionals who may be members of the advisory group can be a valuable source of information about a site's comparative advantage over others in the area.

DEMANDS OF VISITORS

Information on the number of visitors and their likes, dislikes, motivations and expectations will help the planner divide visitors into subgroups of people with similar characteristics, needs and spending behaviours. This information is useful in setting objectives for infrastructure, personnel needs and education and interpretation programmes. Combined with data on tourism markets, the information can be used to develop objectives for attracting certain types of tourists to a site. For example, managers with a policy of boosting local community development might set a goal of attracting tour operators who use local guides.

Numbers of visitors also affect management objectives and infrastructure and facility design. The experience at Liffey Falls in Tasmania illustrates the usefulness of information about visitor preferences when setting management objectives. The Forestry Commission discovered that visitors wanted to see the falls and were not interested in the other available recreation facilities. Knowing this, officials were able to concentrate their efforts and save a considerable amount of money and staff time. At Uluru National Park in Australia, a survey found that most tourists mainly wanted to see and to climb Ayers Rock. Fewer cited experiencing the outback and seeing wildlife as prime reasons for visiting. This information helped park staff to focus their attention on Ayers Rock.

Existing sources can be used to start the process of assessing visitor preferences and demand. Information and statistics from the tourism ministry, protected area staff and tour operators can help provide an idea of current and future demand and the mix of market segments. National tourism officials have information on tourism development and studies or statistics on tourism markets. Statistics and reports from the site staff and tour operators can provide an idea of visitor preferences and demand.

Existing studies from national tourism officials can provide information on the kinds of tourists the government is attempting to attract and the type of tourist expected to visit a site in the future. Interviews with retired parks, forestry or archaeological survey officials may shed light on past management plans and visitation records. Records may include statistics on the number of park visitors, their country of origin and the number of days they spend in the area. Through discussions, officials can help managers identify changes in visitor interests, activities and travel patterns.

A look at tourism development in neighbouring communities can indicate a site's potential demand and show how tourism has affected the economies and social conditions of the community. Local guides and hotel and pen sion owners can provide information on visitor preferences and demand cycles. Also, because they are in constant touch with changes in the international travel markets, they can help in identifying and tracking user preferences and demand, for example, whether visitors travel in tours or organised groups or travel independently. They can provide helpful information for developing infrastructure and interpretation material. Scientists and archaeologists can also share information about visitor preferences and patterns.

Observations, surveys and interviews provide more detailed visitor profiles. Such information on visitors and their interests may be needed to fine-tune management objectives, for example, on crowding preferences or tourists' spending patterns. Observations are qualitative and less exact than surveys and interviews, but they are quick, inexpensive and useful for indicating trends or suggesting targets for an eventual survey or interview. Observations may include: organisation (group size), forms of transportation, type and amount of equipment, uses of time, maps of where people go and behaviour including languages used and noise levels. Since most people have difficulty analysing their own behaviour and motivations, observations can be a quick and useful technique for monitoring what people actually do.

Surveys are less expensive than face-to-face interviews, can reach a broad range of visitors and can provide valuable quantitative data, which is useful for reinforcing management decisions. However, with surveys communication is only one-way, and they require skills in questionnaire design and data management. They are also less effective than interviews in educating visitors. Ideally, a combination of methods should be used to determine preferences and construct accurate visitor profiles. Categorising tourists according to preferences and behaviours can contribute to the realisation of a site's goals and objectives. For example, if income generation is a key goal, information should be compiled on variations in spending by visitors. If education of schoolchildren is a priority, they should figure in a survey.

SOLUTIONS TO MANAGEMENT PROBLEMS

Direct management actions confront problems of human behaviour through regulations that may entail enforcement, restricting activities or rationing use. Indirect methods seek to affect behaviour through education, information and persuasion. Visitors can be informed about the impacts connected with a certain activity, or given information that encourages the use of certain areas over threatened areas. Other indirect actions include physical alterations, such as the redirection of a trail to a more resilient area of a forest, that influence the movement of visitors. In general, indirect actions are more successful in remote areas, where visitors' freedom to explore is usually a primary goal. Direct approaches are often used to prohibit visitors from entering fragile or dangerous areas, for example at an archaeological site where they might damage a priceless fresco.

Experts say regulations succeed when they have strong public support, are carefully explained, and when visitors have some say in how they are implemented. Visitors must understand why a behaviour change is desirable. Once implemented, of course, regulations must be enforced. In practice, a combination of methods is generally used. For example, both direct and indirect actions can be used to minimise visitors' impact on a coral reef. Site staff can design an extensive public information campaign that can include printed materials, direct advertising and school programmes. Tour operators can be managed through permits, regulations and enforcement actions aimed at concentrating recreation activities at resistant reefs.

A combination of methods is also recommended for controlling vandalism, including physical protection of the resource as well as education, making a site inaccessible to vehicles, increasing admission fees and protecting sites by not promoting them. Management strategies should be in line with objectives. For example, if a management objective at a Himalayan site is to offer visitors the freedom to explore, then a softer management approach may be appropriate. Here staff may wish to emphasise educating rekkers on low-impact expedition behaviour. On the other hand, if a site's objective is to protect a priceless mosaic at an ancient monument, a more direct approach may be appropriate such as the deployment of guards to protect the site from looters or vandals and to regulate tourism activity near the work of art.

Before taking actions that may face resistance, it is important to ensure that norms and regulations give managers the legal mandate to act, and that appropriate enforcement systems will support its application. Awareness of the visitor profile helps to ensure success. For example, a large group of foreign visitors may be strongly motivated towards the protection of an endangered species but unaware that they are disturbing the animal during feeding times. In this case, educational materials explaining low-impact viewing techniques may be the best method for minimising impacts. Actions should be relatively easy and inexpensive to implement. In general, direct methods are considered more time-consuming and costly, while indirect actions are thought to be cheaper in the long run.

The most effective but least restrictive management actions should be implemented first. The results should be monitored, and more restrictive actions may be implemented if necessary until conditions improve. For example, to deal with uncontrolled dumping of garbage, an educational campaign may be launched describing the problem and inviting voluntary compliance with a regulation against dumping at the site. If voluntary methods fail, a fine can be imposed. If this doesn't work, the area may have to be closed. At some sites, human and financial resource limitations may necessitate more direct approaches in the short term. Experts in both the North and the South stress the need to develop visitor education programmes and other indirect methods. However, managers often opt for direct methods when faced with problems such as proximity to high population centres and limited staff and finances. In these situations, the cost and time involved in implementing indirect methods is weighed against immediate problems, such as the need to prevent the rapid degradation of an archaeological site by visitors buying objects stolen from the site.

Reducing Crowd in High Use Areas

Reducing visitation in high use areas is a justifiable means of avoiding social impacts such as crowding, but may not by itself substantially reduce some ecological impacts. Reducing the number of people in an area can effectively reduce crowding or congestion, for example at a historical monument. Also, where light use causes considerable environmental damage, decreases in traffic in the area may not have correspondingly positive effects. In such cases reducing visitor traffic may do little to boost recovery rates for soil and vegetation and an area may need to be closed for recovery to occur. On sites that have already suffered degradation to vegetation, practically all use may have to be curtailed before recovery can occur. Impacts to water and wildlife resources are more varied and in some cases can respond to a reduction in use levels. For example, bears in the Yellowstone National Park World Heritage site pose a greater problem in high-use areas, and reducing visitation may reduce incidents between bears and campers.

In some areas, even if limits are imposed, measures to concentrate and control visitors are needed to reduce ecological impacts. People have a tendency to go to the same places and follow the same routes. However, once people arrive at an established site such as a camping ground, they tend to disperse within the limits of the camping area. Limiting use-for example by reducing the number of campsites around a lake-would reduce the number of visitors but not necessarily reduce their ecological impact as they spread out over all the campsites. Actions would be needed to both reduce the number of people and ensure the permanent closing of selected campsites. On the other hand, in lightly used areas, visitor reductions can minimise ecological impacts as long as use levels are kept low, visitors are instructed in low-impact techniques and they avoid fragile areas. Even one uneducated party of visitors can inflict serious damage.

Limiting the length of stay at a site can reduce numbers and alleviate crowding problems but may not necessarily reduce environmental impacts. Limits can be placed on time spent anywhere at the site or at specific areas, a measure that helps reduce crowding. Length-of-stay limits at heavily used natural areas are unlikely to have any effect on ecological impacts unless the limits are very restrictive and targeted to reduce measurable indicators. Ecological impacts are best reduced by imposing length-of-stay limits in lightly used areas; in fragile areas, a long stay in any one place could cause unacceptable impacts.

Closing an area can be an effective way to protect or restore environmental quality. The measure encourages the recovery of vegetation and reduces wildlife impacts. For example, visitors to Big Bend National Park in Texas, USA, are excluded during the breeding season of peregrine falcons to protect their nesting sites. Closure of an area, however, is a direct action that can be controversial and have economic and social ramifications. Any closure should be explained to the local community, not just to would-be visitors.

Reducing numbers by limiting the size of parties can also help control ecological and social impacts. Large parties can cause overcrowding as well as visitor conflicts. In more popular areas, limits on party size and an educational campaign may be needed to reduce impacts and to ensure more privacy for each group of visitors. In such cases educational programmes should stress the importance of using existing areas and keeping them pleasant for the next visitors. Big groups are likely to create wider disturbed areas than smaller groups because they tend to spread out over a larger area. They can also disturb an area more rapidly than a small party. However in an area that is already heavily affected, it makes little difference if a group size is 10 or 50.

Quotas can be used to reduce visitor levels but raise several issues. A point to consider is the financial cost of implementing and administering the quota system. If staffing is insufficient, a quota system probably cannot be maintained over the long term. Also, quotas favour people who can book in advance, excluding other categories of potential visitors. Any sort of limitation may annoy visitors who cherish their freedom. Quota systems may especially irk those who consider themselves traditional users of a site. As a result they may choose to go elsewhere, and other sites may not be able to cope with increased use. Thus, for a quota system to be successful, access should be limited to alternative sites and user groups need to understand and accept the rationing technique being implemented.

Increasing visitor fees and other charges can reduce visitor numbers. The laws of supply and demand dictate that higher fees at a site will reduce visitation. A factor to consider when raising fees is the elasticity of demand, or how sensitive visitors are to a change in the cost of entering an area. This information can be gleaned from surveys. Another factor to consider is that visitors want pricing schemes to be easy and straightforward. They tend to prefer an all-inclusive fee over a main fee plus separate charges such as for parking or taking photographs. Setting visitor fees may also involve setting different entrance fees' for local people and foreigners.

Not providing facilities can reduce visitor numbers. Limiting infrastructure such as camping areas or parking spaces can reduce visitor numbers just as adding infrastructure can increase numbers. Simply making access more difficult, for instance, by locating parking farther away from entrances, can also slow visitation. In Costa Rica, community pressure to limit tourism at a Reserve put a stop to a plan to pave the access road to the community and the reserve. On the other hand, increasing infrastructure such as adding signs and informational plaques can increase the popularity of a site and its resources, for example, an underwater shipwreck. This strategy raises several issues including safety concerns. At a rain forest park, for example, management may want to provide a system of signs, boardwalks and bridges to direct visitors safely back to the entrance rather than run the risk of having to carry out expensive searchand-rescue operations. The elasticity of demand related to infrastructure development may vary from one site to another. Many World Heritage sites, because they are unique, can attract significant numbers of people even if infrastructure development is limited. By maintaining ongoing dialogue with stakeholders such as tour operators who are members of the site's tourism advisory board and who have an intimate knowledge of visitor preferences and movements, site managers can obtain practical advice on the effects of these policies.

Concentrating Tourists

Concentrating people can limit social and environmental impacts. The strategy offers a high level of control and protection for sensitive resources: By limiting use to a few selected areas within a site, particularly areas that are resistant to impacts or at least not as sensitive to impacts, the policy confines disturbance to a smaller area. So at sites with sensitive resources, a concentration strategy can be used to direct visitors to areas where resources are more resilient and resistant. For example, some corals are more resistant to impacts than others, so visitors may be concentrated at more resistant areas. At Stonehenge, except for certain religious groups who are free to enter at certain times, visitors are not permitted to cross the site's outer perimeter. Besides limiting impacts to certain areas, concentrating use may open up new opportunities. For example, the policy may provide a rare opportunity to experience an area in relative isolation, perhaps at an archaeological site.

The chance to be part of a small group visiting an isolated, highly protected site may be unique, and one that people may also be willing to pay more for. A policy of concentrating may help avert possible impacts on naturally fragile areas resulting from the tendency of tourism enterprises such as hotel chains and theme parks to grow and expand. In sites that are already heavily impacted, there may be no other alternative but to encourage or restrict visitors to existing use patterns. Since people tend to use the same areas and the same routes, implementing this measure is usually not difficult and can be accomplished through regulation or through indirect methods such as persuading visitors to use a certain area or providing infrastructure in specific areas.

Concentrating tourists may produce a positive social outcome by allowing local people to escape the pressures associated with tourism. For example, in community rural village encampments developed for tourists in Senegal, tourist accommodations are situated well away from the village centre. In Ujung Kulon National Park in West Java in Indonesia, tourism activities are restricted to a zone that is managed by a private company that provides accommodation and services. A possible disadvantage of concentrating use is that it changes the social climate of an environment for the visitors. At many sites, when tourists are clustered together, for example in an enclave of small hotels, they lose the feeling of solitude. This may be contrary to the visitor experience that was originally planned and/or what originally attracted people to the site.

Limiting environmental impacts in natural areas by dispersing use to different areas can be effective in areas where use levels are low and visitors are conscientious about their behaviour. A dispersal policy should be supported with programmes designed to control where people go and how they engage in recreational activities. The policy may not be feasible at natural sites with limited resources for educating or controlling visitors. In addition, careful monitoring of a dispersal programme is needed because of the high potential for spreading problems.

Dispersing visitors by extending the tourist season is an option that may have ecological consequences. For example, using quotas and visitor permits can reduce crowding but may concentrate use in a season during which vegetation and wildlife are more fragile. Wildlife is especially vulnerable during the reproductive months and when animals feed for winter. During periods of higher rainfall and snowmelt, the ground may be more susceptible to compaction and breaking. Plants are more vulnerable during growth seasons.

At cultural sites, such as monuments with well-developed and protective infrastructure where there is little risk of environmental impacts, dispersing visitors is an effective way to relieve crowding. Dispersing visitors to different areas of a site can be accomplished through regulations or through information and persuasion. It can also be accomplished through the strategic placement of infrastructure. If staffing levels allow, direct actions such as issuing permits may also be effective. A permit system increases the distance between parties and supports a management objective of providing an experience in which human encounters are infrequent.

The decision to concentrate or disperse tourism should reflect policy goals and management objectives. A frequent policy goal is to assure that the benefits of tourism flow to the communities around a site. This may lead to pressure to open up new areas of a site to visitors. Tourism has a tendency to spread, and can lead in turn to the spread of social and ecological impacts. If on the other hand local economic development is a key goal, and there is sufficient revenue-generating potential to replace current economic activities in a given area, then expanding tourism to the area may be appropriate. But if the main policy goal is protection of an endangered species and promoting visits by biologists, expanding tourism within a park may limit opportunities for research because of increased tourism impacts in sensitive areas.

Strengthening the Durability of Physical Environment

Increasing a site's resistance to visitor impacts by installing or modifying infrastructure is generally referred to as site-hardening. Adding infrastructure, or "hardening" a site, strengthens its physical durability. This may involve surfacing access routes and trails, or building shelters for trekkers, or barriers to prevent people from touching priceless mosaics such as at the Taj Mahal. An example of extensive hardening of a cultural site is at the Great Temple of Abu Simbel, in Egypt, where the daily influx of 2,000 tourists was causing traffic jams. Inside the temple, their respiration increased the humidity and carbon dioxide in the air, causing salt deposits to form on the walls. To address the traffic problems, management implemented a one-way road system. A ventilation system was installed to reduce the humidity and the temperature in the burial chamber. Another way to avoid impacts is simply to move infrastructure away from sensitive areas.

Hardening has both costs and benefits because it changes the nature of the visitors' experience. Hardening can lead to a change in visitor profile. The Milford track in New Zealand and the Overland track in Tasmania, both popular backpacking routes, saw an increase in use during the 1980s. Management responded to the resulting impacts by rationing use and hardening the tracks surfaces. Consequently, some visitors considered the tracks too easy and stopped using them. Making experiences easier by hardening a site can also increase the level of crowding. In Tasmania, a boardwalk was built to restrict access to parts of the Gorden River. For business reasons, tour group sizes were not reduced, and groups could number more than 50. Crowding onto the boardwalk, the visitors had difficulty photographing one of the site's star attractions, a famous 2,000-year-old Huon pine tree. Another effect of site hardening is that added materials may not blend in with the surrounding environment, compromising the original values of the site. One solution is to use natural materials instead of intrusive man-made materials. For example, fast-growing plants can be used to block a trail leading to a fragile or restricted area, or an entrance may be filled in with natural debris and rocks.

Visitor's Behaviour Changing

Interpretation and education programmes can mitigate environmental and social impacts. Educational programmes instruct people on how best to behave at a site. Interpretation programmes inform and explain the site's resources and significance to the visitor. Visitors can be taught low-impact techniques at both cultural and natural sites. In the United States, a "Save the Manatee Campaign" involved distributing guidelines to tourists and resulted in a decline in manatee mortality and injury. At the Luxor site, in Egypt, authorities reported that by explaining management problems to visitors they succeeded in distributing visitor movements more evenly. Interpretation and education programmes, although they may take time to succeed, may be preferable to infrastructure development because they are less likely to change the visitor experience and displace original target groups.

Certain impacts can be almost eliminated by teaching visitors minimum-impact techniques. In Tasmania, on the Overland track in the Cradle Mountain-Lake St. Clair National Park, trekkers came down with gastroenteritis because they were burying their waste too close to camping huts, contaminating water and food supplies. At one point up to half of the users were reporting falling ill. To correct the situation, park management mailed materials to walking clubs, environmental groups and camping stores outlining the problem and the solution that walkers bury their waste at least 100 metres from huts, campsites and streams. The following summer, only eight to 10 percent of the users reported contracting gastroenteritis. Similar results have been achieved with education campaigns promoting low-impact wildlife viewing and other ecologically sound practices such as using stoves instead of fires, packing out garbage and not feeding animals. Most experts in the protection of monuments also advocate visitor education as part of the strategy for combatting problems such as vandalism.

Interpretation and education campaigns need not be overly costly. Goals should be critically evaluated to determine whether they could be met just as effectively through modest means. Instead of allocating huge sums to large infrastructure projects such as sophisticated visitor centres, cheaper approaches may be more effective, for example, a programme involving personal contact between visitors and management staff. In some situations a team could travel from site to site to update and improve interpretation facilities and materials, and to train local managers and rangers. Educational and interpretation campaigns are possible at minimal expense. For example on a short nature walk, small signs giving the common and scientific names of the flora can suffice, while larger signs can be made on more general themes.

Changing visitor behaviour is not a simple process. Interpretation and education campaigns stem from a desire to change visitor behaviour, a simple principle in theory but complex in practice. Many factors have been found to influence visitor behaviour, including the following: Visitors want to know why they should do something. A simple statement that an area is a low-use area does not provide enough information. The interpretation programme must match the current reality, or confusion will result. For example, photographs and descriptions in promotional publications may not correspond to the visitor experience.

Feedback from visitors revealed that they had not expected to be able to see clearcutting from trails and picnic areas. One solution was to include images of forest production activities in the promotional literature. The behaviour of staff including maintenance personnel must uphold the values reflected in educational and interpretation materials. A visitor's experience and prior knowledge may influence the effectiveness of educational materials. Research has indicated that educational materials are more effective for visitors with limited experience of a site or advance information about it.

Special care must be taken with the content and delivery of interpretation materials for repeat visitors. Experts recommend that if two versions of the materials are not feasible it may be better to ignore the more experienced audience.

Visitors must believe that a given issue is real and serious, that a given action is necessary, and that they can make a difference. Materials should present an issue along with information on how to address it, linking visitors' experience with future actions. The materials could include information on environmentalists' clubs, other places to visit and learn about a subject, or other additional information. A person has to believe that he or she is capable of contributing to a solution, such as by planting a seedling in a reforestation project or helping out at an archaeological dig. Individual rewards can be financial but "psychic rewards" the gratification deriving from altruistic motives are often more meaningful.

Several other factors figure in the effective presentation of interpretation and educational programmes. Clear goals and objectives are needed to determine what is to be interpreted, for whom and how, and who will develop interpretation strategies. The crucial step of identifying fundamental messages and target audiences is reportedly the weakest link in the process of developing interpretation concepts and themes. Materials should focus on the type of visitor whose behaviour is considered most in need of change. The message should clearly describe the critical problems and recommended behaviours.

The most effective educational campaigns use a combination of methods tailored for particular user groups and messages. They are based on specific visitor profiles cataloguing age, background, interests, origin (foreign or local), degree of skill in the activities the site offers, special needs, form of access to the site (road or waterway, public or private). Profiles also take into account whether visitors are on their own, in couples or families, or part of an organised group.

Interpretation criteria may change with societal changes such as shifts in ethnicity or local education levels. Such shifts may necessitate new messages, perhaps in different languages. An exhibit should satisfy the expectations of occasional tourists as well as those of local residents and repeat visitors. Layered signs offer detailed information in smaller print intended to pique the interest of repeat visitors.

Studies show the need for careful analysis of visitor interests. Many people visit World Heritage sites out of a general interest in heritage. Most visitors to World Heritage sites have little specialist knowledge or interest; the particulars of a castle or other historical site are of secondary importance. Interpretative programmes should be evaluated in terms of whether they are meeting management goals and objectives. If not, they are a poor investment of scarce resources, at the expense of other programmes and the management's reputation. Experts warn against a tendency to produce new programmes rather than re-examine existing ones, leaving no arguments in favour of one or the other. The easiest and most common way to evaluate the effectiveness of an interpretation programme such as an exhibit is to assess its ability to attract and hold visitors' attention.

In this case an exhibit is judged on how many people stop and how much time they spend looking and/or reading the exhibit material. Staff intuition concerning attitude change is generally reliable and can contribute to assessment studies. The target audience may be reached in various ways, depending on the type of materials used. In general, visitors who must rely on public transport or a service provided by the site management for access to an area is a captive audience.

Staff can inform visitors of park regulations and provide safety advice and orientation pointers. To encourage return visits, exhibits should be changed regularly, or special exhibitions should be staged on occasion. Guides can be invaluable in imparting educational information to visitors. In large tropical rain forests, for example, tourists unaccompanied by an excellent guide may spend long periods without seeing any wildlife. Eighty to 95 percent of travellers to rain forest lodges in one region of Peru reported being unsatisfied with wildlife viewing. Involving guides in the planning stages when developing educational and interpretation programmes helps to ensure consistency in visitor information. Guides and site staff should liaise closely so that guides do not compete with the aims of the site, and so that their information is correct and consistent.

Methods of presentation vary in their ability to attract visitors and change behaviour. The following materials have been found to be effective. The Tasmania Parks Department found that the most effective presentation materials were fun as well as easy and quick to read. Videos were the most popular and the most effective. Because videos bring information to life and show how techniques work in practice, they are popular for use in schools and with inexperienced groups.

Comic posters, audio-visual materials and multimedia presentations have also proven effective. Once materials raise visitors' attention, the most effective method for changing behaviours is to add personal contact. For example, walkers are more readily convinced not to use stoves when rangers inform them face to face about regulations, reinforcing a strong educational campaign. Simply erecting signs saying "fuel stoves only" is far less effective. In the absence of rangers, guides can be trained to present interpretation information. Workshops for commercial tour guides could cover low-impact techniques and other management issues. Local guides at Nan Madol, a South Pacific island with an important archaeological site, are crucial in educating tourists and controlling graffiti and other forms of vandalism.

Interactive interpretive programmes show great promise. Participatory exhibits are more popular than static displays and are highly effective in changing visitor behaviour. Active participation seems to foster a positive attitude, especially when combined with a rewarding experience. Interactive techniques giving opportunities for feedback include despatching roving staff or placing them at fixed points to provide information; holding conferences or discussions; offering entertainment events such as puppet shows, plays or musicals, or organising activities such as making and measuring things, games and re-enactments of historical events.

Publications, signs, self-guided activities, visitor centres, audio-visual devices, indoor and outdoor exhibitions such as walks, drives and snorkelling trails in marine parks are less interactive-but less timeconsuming for staff. Hands-on workshops may be coupled with field trips and observational tours. One scientist-teacher from Puerto Rico recommended that coastal ecosystems are best understood through field trips during which participants can question and interact with the expert. The Tropen Museum in Amsterdam offers a programme in which people can seek advice from experienced travellers about current events in a particular country and various cultural do's and don'ts.

Authentic displays based on economic activities using real artefacts and materials are increasingly popular. At the National Fishing Centre in Grimsby, England, for example, former trawler hands recount their experiences to the public and encourage participation by instructing visitors in knotting fishing line. Heritage centres increasingly offer authentic experiences through imaginative interpretations of local history. Since the 1980s, old established museums, thanks to new technologies, have been offering entertainment as well as education, blurring the distinction between the theme park and museum experience.

Oral history is a particularly useful research asset and an important source of interpretative material. The process gets local people involved and makes them feel represented, which may be especially important if it turns out that the local interpretation is at variance with that of site materials. Including the voices of local people in interpretative programmes gives them a central role, encouraging popular support.

Regulating Visitor Activity

Regulations limiting activities and/or the way they are practised can radically affect ecological and social impacts. Some recreation activities produce more impacts than others. The types of visitor activities can be limited. For example, banning off-road vehicles and motorcycles reduces soil erosion, as does the use of horses. To limit traffic and pollution problems, Bermuda has adopted a policy of not recognising foreign drivers' licences, making car rental impossible. Similarly, non-resident cars have been banned on the Italian islands of Capri, Ischia and Procida. To minimise negative impacts due to encounters between tourists and whales at Glacier Bay, Alaska, authorities have set limits on the number of cruise ships entering the bay and issued regulations for maintaining a minimum distance of 400 metres between ships and whales. Whalewatching regulations are also in place for local guides at Viscaino Bay in Baja, California. Once again, such regulatory measures require sufficient resources to implement. Complementary indirect actions can provide support to direct actions. For example, at some game parks in Africa, drivers often fail to observe regulations for maintaining acceptable distances from the wildlife. To address this problem, culverts can be dug alongside roads to prevent vehicles from leaving them.

Allocating specific activities to certain areas helps reduce conflict between different types of visitors. For example, groups such as snorkellers and sports fishermen would conflict if they tried to use the same areas. The concept of separating user groups is related to the Recreational Opportunity Spectrum. A key issue when using this technique is to ensure that the different areas for different activities remain in good environmental condition for the long term. Visitors and tour operators could be informed that if an area allocated to them is damaged, they won't be offered an alternative area.

Developing interpretation and education programmes in close cooperation with the community can help to avoid alienating local people who may otherwise feel their cultural identity is being misrepresented. The feeling of sense of place and the strong spirituality and identity which traditional people have for their land is not easily conveyed to visitors. For the local community, memory, attachment and symbolism are often of primary importance. In contrast, visitors may seem to diminish local values by being attracted to the unfamiliar, exotic and picturesque. Interpretation and education programmes, when developed in close cooperation with the community, can help prevent a devaluation of traditional local values.

Locals are more likely to participate in conservation when it is associated with an improvement in their standard of living. Managers at Ujung Kulon National Park in West Java in Indonesia report that local income-generating activities in tourism, resource management and protection encourage local support for park protection and conservation efforts. Environmental conservation and education programmes alone will not achieve results. In Gambia, West Africa, the local community's acceptance of the new Kiang West National Park was based entirely on the expectation that they would receive a portion of the economic benefits of tourism.

However, increasing local benefits-for example, by providing training for local guides-does not necessarily draw people into conservation and protection activities. Experience has shown that conservation and economic development should be linked. Thus guides should be recruited who have an ongoing interest in conservation or community participation. Evaluations of local guide training in Costa Rica indicated a need for a comprehensive selection process, in search of both talent and environmental and community consciousness.

Experience has determined that community tourism projects are sustainable when people invest their labour and savings in them. Projects succeed when people have a stake in them. When people can see the project's benefits they willingly contribute their labour or money. In Nepal's Annapurna Conservation Area Project, people are expected to contribute cash or labour to community development projects. Lodge owners who upgrade their facilities are provided with technical assistance and training including help in the development of their standards.

Community tourism programmes may be more effective if introduced gradually and in conjunction with other economic development programmes. Gradual introduction is recommended in view of potential negative social and economic impacts. Communities may need time to adapt to the realities of the industry, to manage problems stemming from the influx of visitors, and to plan efficient ways to capture and retain economic benefits from tourism. A community's expectations of

economic benefits are often disappointed because of
inadequate local conditions. For example, foreign tourists
may demand standards of accommodations and food
beyond what the local community can immediately
provide. Thus, locals may not begin to see direct
economic benefits until certain basic problems are
addressed. Gradual implementation can exacerbate the
problem, as people become impatient for the economic
benefits. Such problems may be mitigated when other
incomegenerating programmes are carried ·out
concurrently and the community is not oriented solely
towards tourism. For example, many projects at protected
areas include agroforestry and other resource
development programmes that can produce economic
benefits such as crops and wood lots for firewood. Such
options can lessen the need for more rapid tourism
development.

Tourism's potential for benefiting locals is a function
of the existing resources and skills that can be used to
generate income. Community tourism programmes
should start with an evaluation of local resources and
skills with which activities can be matched. For example,
in many instances local transportation support is needed
for tourism activities, or local knowledge is in demand
because of difficult terrain, such as at Corcovado National
Park in Costa Rica, where ground transportation to the
park is difficult, and flying is more expensive. Other
activities that may need local guiding and transportation
skills include mountaineering, trekking, sport fishing,
skin diving, and horseback riding. More specialised
activities such as bird-watching and river rafting usually
require more education and training. Opportunities for
these activities often depend on the existence of
government or NGO training programmes, and tour
operators who are interested in involving local people.

Labour costs should be realistically evaluated when
analysing community potential. If little or no capital is

required to develop a guesthouse, for example, where rooms formerly occupied by children are converted into rooms for guests, the project may be attractive. Also, if the time spent on tourism enterprises could not be better spent on other pursuits, for example, if few work opportunities exist other than in tourism, then a community tourism project may be worthwhile even if the pay is low.

Experience has shown that tourism often fails to generate local economic benefits when local guides are under-utilised. Tour companies and hotels tend not to use local guides. In some countries and in specific protected areas, they are required to use under-skilled local guides, which they often see as a financial drain. This problem may be mitigated through intensive training of local guides in language and interpretation skills. Guides with better skills are more readily accepted by tourist businesses. As tour operators and governments realise that site protection and the health of the tourist trade depend on local support, they begin to see that it is in their interests to support the hiring and training of local people.

Raising site revenue to produce local benefits. The costs and benefits of infrastructure and high-tech solutions should be reviewed in light of the goal of producing local benefits. Planners at the Copan Maya Ruins in the Honduras realised that luxury hotels tend to be located away from population centres, limiting opportunities for locals. Noting that most domestic visitors have modest financial resources and prefer local accommodations, they recommended upgrading existing infrastructure and related services. They also deemed that concentrated, modest, but good quality tourist facilities could provide many more benefits to local communities than high-class, high-cost hotels, restaurants and guide services. Such services often use outside labour, are controlled by outside capital, and are intentionally located outside local communities. High-tech solutions to management problems should not be adopted without a serious review of their costs, benefits and applicability on the ground. In some countries where unemployment is already high, these measures can put even more people out of work.

It may be advisable and just as effective, for example, to use local labour to build and maintain palm thatch roofs to protect stone artefacts from deterioration instead of using chemical compounds. By the same token, power lawnmowers are obviously more efficient than manual labour for cutting grass, but lawnmowers need spare parts that may have to be imported. Visitor fees can generate benefits for both protected areas and local communities. Most studies on protected area management recommend government policies authorising the collection of fees to offset costs.

Fees can be charged for admission to parks or monuments, and for different activities such as diving and trekking, and for accommodation and rescue services. User fees are equitable because the people who use the site pay for it. Fees for public areas such as parks or museums are kept low to permit access to a greater cross-section of the population. To capture more foreign exchange and increase revenues, some sites charge a higher rate for foreign tourists than for nationals.

In countries where such a two-tier system is illegal, donations can be solicited from foreign tourists and tour companies. It should be noted that a chronic problem for many sites that collect fees is that the money is returned to a central treasury and does not go to site operations. Experts report that the tourism industry may resist visitor charges even though visitors may be willing to pay more for entrance fees. Visitors tend to accept fee increases if they know the funds will go to site protection and conservation. They want to know where the money goes. Visitor preference data could be collected in support of a fee increase that may be opposed by certain stakeholders. Concession fees charged to individuals or groups licensed to provide services to visitors can also generate revenues both for sites and local communities. Common concessions include food, lodging, transport, guide and retail services. Concession fees and royalties can generate significant income at highly visited sites. Since concession fees are generally low relative to overall profit levels, businesses may be willing to pay higher fees.

CHAPTER 5

COMMUNITY-BASED TOUR OPERATION

Community Based Tourism (CBT) is a unique type of tourism with characteristics quite different from mass tourism. Those who intend to put CBT into practice need to fully understand the underlying ideas, principles and components behind CBT. CBT is not simply a tourism business that aims at maximizing profits for investors. Rather, it is more concerned with the impact of tourism on the community and environmental resources.

CBT emerges from a community development strategy, using tourism as a tool to strengthen the ability of rural community organizations that manage tourism resources with the participation of the local people. However, CBT is far from a perfect, prepackaged solution to community problems. Nor is it a miracle cure or a knight in shining armor that will come to save the community. In fact, if carelessly applied, CBT can cause problems and bring disaster. For this reason, communities that are appropriate for the development of CBT must be chosen carefully and adequately prepared before operating CBT. More importantly, the community should have the strength to modify or suspend CBT, should it grow beyond the management capacity of the community or bring unmanageable negative impacts.

The principles listed below present the concept of CBT, and the way the host community can use tourism as a tool for community development. CBT should:

1. Recognize, support and promote community ownership of tourism;

2. Involve community members from the start in every aspect;

3. Promote community pride;

4. Improve the quality of life;

5. Ensure environmental sustainability;

6. Preserve the unique character and culture of the local area;

7. Foster cross-cultural learning;

8. Respect cultural differences and human dignity;

9. Distribute benefits fairly among community members;

10. Contribute a fixed percentage of income to community projects.

Before developing CBT in line with these principles, it is necessary to prepare and build the capacity of the host community to manage tourism. CBT marketing should also promote public awareness of the differences between CBT and mass tourism, educating people to realize the importance of CBT as a community tool for resource conservation and cultural preservation. This will attract appropriate tourists for CBT.

Tourism in which the community plays a role goes by a great variety of names: 'Community Based Tourism' (CBT), 'Community Based Ecotourism' (CBET), 'Agrotourism', 'Eco' and 'Adventure Tourism' and 'Homestay' are a few of the prominent terms. Among academics worldwide, there is not yet any consensus on terms for various types of tourism.

KEY ELEMENTS OF CBT

CBT is tourism that takes environmental, social, and cultural sustainability into account. It is managed and owned by the community, for the community, with the purpose of enabling visitors to increase their awareness and learn about the community and local ways of life.The following are the key elements of CBT:

Natural and Cultural Resources

— Natural resources are well preserved
— Local economy and modes of production depend on the sustainable use of natural resources
— Customs and culture are unique to the destination

Community Organizations

— The Community shares consciousness, norms and ideology
— The Community has elders who hold local traditional knowledge and wisdom.
— The Community has a sense of ownership and wants to participate in its own development

Management

— The Community has rules and regulations for environmental, cultural, and tourism management.
— A local organization or mechanism exists to manage tourism with the ability to link tourism and community development.
— Benefits are fairly distributed to all.
— A percentage of profits from tourism is contributed to a community fund for economic and social development of the community.

Learning

Tourism activities and services aim at:
— Fostering a shared learning process between hosts and guests.

— Educating and building understanding of diverse cultures and ways of life.

— Raising awareness of natural and cultural conservation among tourists and the local community.

CBT AS A TOOL FOR COMMUNITY DEVELOPMENT

CBT is intended as a tool for community development and environmental conservation. For this reason, you should apply a "holistic" view, (i.e., one that encompasses a complete range of social, cultural, economic, environmental and political development factors), to your analysis of the community context. Understanding the community situation will help you maximize the capacity of CBT to act as an effective and sustainable community development strategy.

The impacts of globalized trade and investment on local community development since that time deserve concern and contemplation. Before setting tourism objectives, you should consider the conditions of the relationship between the community and its: natural resources (e.g., rights, conflicts); cultural heritage (e.g., continuity); modernization (e.g., quality of life, consumerism); economic development (e.g., employment and income stability) rights to self-governance (e.g., role of local government, degree of local participation)

CBT and community development are inherently connected, because they share the same natural and cultural resource. Culture and social norms determine not only resource use but also structure internal and external relationships. Ideally, the value of fostering the relationship between Local Cultural Wisdom and Local Environmental Resources should be internalized by the community members and integrated into all aspects of CBT management. Tourism can be a powerful tool for community development, especially if you view tourism and community development as necessarily connected.

In preparing the community for CBT, you should consider the establishment a Contract or Commitment among the stakeholders. This can be done through the process of settling on mutual goals and participating in the ten steps below. Steps 1 and 2 are particularly important before determining to begin CBT. Step 9 is a way to evaluate the readiness of the community to manage tourism.

Although it is important to build the confidence of the community, we did include this as a specific step. The facilitating organization should rather integrate 'community confidence building' throughout the developmental process. Measuring Community Confidence is also an informal way for the facilitating organization to evaluate community capacity to manage CBT. The steps of building community capacity to manage tourism is as follows.

1. Choose a destination.
2. Complete a feasibility study in cooperation with the community
3. Set vision and objectives with the community
4. Develop a plan to prepare the community to manage tourism
5. Set direction for organizational management
6. Design tour programs
7. Train interpretive guides
8. Develop a marketing plan
9. Launch a pilot tour program
10. Monitor and evaluate the process

COMMUNITY-BASED ECOTOURISM

The community-based ecotourism is a form of ecotourism where the local community has substantial control over, and involvement in, its development and management, and a major proportion of the benefits remain within the community. How the community is defined will depend on the social and institutional structures in the area concerned, but the definition implies some kind of collective responsibility and approval by representative bodies. In many places, particularly those inhabited by indigenous peoples, there are collective rights over lands and resources. Community-based ecotourism should therefore foster sustainable use and collective responsibility. However, it must also embrace individual initiatives within the community. Some further general characteristics of ecotourism have been identified by UNEP and the World Tourism Organisation as:

— involving appreciation not only of nature, but also of indigenous cultures prevailing in natural areas, as part of the visitor experience;

— containing education and interpretation as part of the tourist offer;

— generally, but not exclusively, organised for small groups by small, specialised and locally owned businesses;

— minimising negative impacts on the natural and socio-cultural environment;

— supporting the protection of natural areas by generating economic benefits for the managers of natural areas;

— providing alternative income and employment for local communities; and

— increasing local and visitor awareness of conservation.

The processes involved in ecotourism include all aspects of planning, developing, marketing and managing resources and facilities for this form of tourism. Visitor provision includes access to natural areas and cultural heritage, guiding and interpretative services, accommodation, catering, sales of produce and handicrafts, and transport. Appropriate recreational and special interest activities, such as trail walking, photography and participatory conservation programmes, may also be part of ecotourism. In some locations, hunting and fishing may be included as appropriate activities, provided that they are carefully researched and controlled within a management plan that supports conservation. This kind of sustainable use relies on local knowledge, provides significant local income, and encourages communities to place a high value on wildlife, resulting in net conservation benefits.

WWF's Tourism Position Statement states that WWF and the tourism industry should share a common goal: the long-term preservation of the natural environment. It presents a vision that tourism development and practice should:

— be part of a wider sustainable development strategy;

— be compatible with effective conservation of natural ecosystems; and

— involve local people and cultures, ensuring that they have an equitable share in its benefits.

Ecotourism is receiving considerable attention from international and national conservation, development and tourism organisations, such as UNEP and the World Tourism Organisation. At the same time, there has been growing international concern that ecotourism should be genuinely community-based. There are many reported incidents where forms of 'ecotourism', which are not sufficiently community focused, are having a negative impact on the environment, and where indigenous communities are not receiving sufficient benefit.

Moreover, many small scale community-based ecotourism initiatives have been set up which have failed owing to a lack of market assessment, organisation, quality and promotion. Ecotourism is no panacea. It is important not to exaggerate the opportunities and benefits it can bring. Careful planning and improved knowledge is needed. Ecotourism and responsible tourism should be part of wider sustainable development strategies, whether at a community or an international level.

In most ecotourism projects, a fundamental objective is improved conservation of landscapes and biodiversity. Community-based ecotourism should be seen and evaluated as just one tool in achieving this. Its role may be to:

— provide a more sustainable form of livelihood for local communities;

— encourage communities themselves to be more directly involved in conservation; and

— generate more goodwill towards, and local benefit from, conservation measures such as protected areas.

There needs to be clear initial understanding of the relationship between local communities and the use of natural resources in the area concerned. The following are important issues to consider.

1. What actions are currently being taken, and by whom, which are supporting or damaging the environment? A challenge for community-based ecotourism is often one of being seen to benefit sufficient numbers of people in the community to make a difference.

2. What type and level of incentive might be needed to change attitudes and actions in order to achieve worthwhile conservation benefits? Could ecotourism deliver this? How does it compare with other development options which may have worse environmental impacts?

3. What additional problems for conservation might be brought by ecotourism, to set against possible gains? This might include not only development and visitor pressure but also an over-emphasis on certain species compared with biodiversity as a whole.

4. Could alternative sustainable livelihood options achieve the same or better results with less effort or disruption?

The capacity of ecotourism to support a positive attitude towards conservation is not only achieved in proportion to direct economic benefits delivered. With many ecotourism initiatives it has been found that simply raising awareness that there is some realisable value in wildlife and attractive landscapes has been sufficient to make a considerable difference, both within communities and also politically at a regional or national level.

It is important to avoid spending time pursuing ecotourism and raising expectations in circumstances which are highly likely to lead to failure. An initial feasibility assessment should be made before instigating a communitybased strategy. Some preconditions relate to the situation at a national level, others to conditions in the local area. The main aspects to check are as follows. Reasonable conditions for undertaking tourism business are:

— an economic and political framework which does not prevent effective trading and security of investment;

— national legislation which does not obstruct tourism income being earned by and retained within local communities;

— a sufficient level of ownership rights within the local community;

— high levels of safety and security for visitors (both in terms of image of the country/region and in reality);

— relatively low health risks and access to basic medical services and a clean water supply; and

— practicable means of physical access and telecommunication to the area.

Some basic preconditions for community-based ecotourism are:

— landscapes or flora/fauna which have inherent attractiveness or degree of interest to appeal either to specialists or more general visitors;

— ecosystems that are at least able to absorb a managed level of visitation without damage;

— a local community that is aware of the potential opportunities, risks and changes involved, and is interested in receiving visitors;

— existing or potential structures for effective community decision-making;

— no obvious threats to indigenous culture and traditions; and

— an initial market assessment suggesting a potential demand and an effective means of accessing it, and that the area is not over supplied with ecotourism offers.

Some preconditions may be more relevant than others, depending on the local circumstances, and these may change over time. For example, in Namibia cross-border conflict in Caprivi has seriously affected market demand in that region but action is being taken to enable promising ecotourism initiatives there to resume when the situation stabilises. If the preconditions are met, this does not necessarily mean that ecotourism will be successful, only that it is worth proceeding to the next stage of consultation and assessment.Checking these preconditions will require informed judgement. The concept of preconditions and fast pre-feasibility checks is increasingly applied among donor agencies in the tourism field.

Integrated Community Approach to Ecotourism

The small scale of most community-based ecotourism initiatives means that their impact, both on nature conservation and on income and employment for the community as a whole, is limited. They can be more influential and successful if they are integrated within other sustainable development initiatives at a regional and local level.Ecotourism can be integrated with other sectors of the rural economy, creating mutually supportive linkages and reducing financial leakage away from the area. It can also be coordinated with agriculture, in terms of the use of time and resources and in providing markets for local produce. In principle, multiple sector activity within local communities should be encouraged. Ecotourism markets are small, seasonal and sensitive to external influences such as political changes or economic instability in the host or generating country. On the other hand, ecotourism can shield against threats to other sectors.

As well as horizontal integration within the community, the success of local ecotourism initiatives may depend on vertical integration with national level initiatives to support and promote responsible tourism. In addition to making linkages with what may already exist, efforts should be made to influence national policies in favour of ecotourism, including coordination between tourism and environmental ministries and policies. National level support is needed in terms of linking conservation and tourism activities and responsibilities, appropriate legislation and assistance towards small enterprises and community initiatives, and national and international promotion.

Community Involvement

Involving the community is a critically important and complex subject for successful community-based ecotourism. Opportunities and solutions will vary considerably in different areas and between communities. An important principle is to seek to work with existing social and community structures, though these can create challenges as well as opportunities. It can also help to identify potential leaders and people with drive. The main objective should be to achieve broad and equitable benefits throughout the community. Issues of gender may also be important and ecotourism can provide good opportunities for women.

Community-based ecotourism requires an understanding, and where possible a strengthening, of the legal rights and responsibilities of the community over land, resources and development. This should apply in particular to the tenure of community-held lands and to rights over tourism, conservation and other uses on these lands, enabling the community to influence activity and earn income from tourism. It should also apply to participation in land use planning and development control over private property.

It is important to remember that ecotourism is a business. As well as community-led initiatives, private enterprise and investment should be encouraged where appropriate, within a structure which enables the community to benefit, and have decision-making power over the level and nature of tourism in its area. There are various ways in which the community can relate to private enterprise. The degree of community involvement and benefit can develop over time. For example, there are some ecotourism initiatives in the Amazon where lodges, that have been built with private investment, offer a concession to the community, an agreement to hand the business over to them after a specified period, and provision for an employment and training programme for local people.

Options for community involvement with enterprise include the following.

1. Private tourism businesses employing local people. Although a useful form of employment, it is very important to guard against poor wages and conditions and to ensure that training is offered to local people, including in management.

2. Local individuals selling produce and handicraft to visitors directly or through tourism businesses. This has often proved to be a good way of spreading benefits within a community.

3. Private tourism businesses (internally or externally owned) being granted a concession to operate by the community, in return for a fee and a share of revenue. There are many examples where this has worked well.

4. Individuals, with links to the broader community, running their own small tourism businesses. Success can vary and lack of skill and tourism knowledge has often proved a weakness.

5. Communally owned and run enterprises. Sometimes these suffer from lack of organisation and incentive, but this can be overcome with time. Action can be taken to strengthen relationships between the community and private partners. This includes:

    — advice and training for communities on their rights and negotiating practies;

    — ensuring transparent, simple and consistently applied deals give sufficient incentive to private enterprises, recognise commercial realities, and minimise administrative burdens and uncertainty; and

— establishing committees involving local people, private operators and possibly government agencies and NGOs, to ensure understanding and smooth operation of agreements, and to help local communication. The method of distribution of income earned by communities to individual members needs careful attention. This can sometimes be covered in legislation relating to communal rights. There are examples where communally-earned income from ecotourism has been directly divided between households or placed in community development funds or separate trusts for use on community projects such as health or education programmes.

Community-based Ecotourism Strategy

All community-based ecotourism initiatives should be centred on a clear strategy agreed and understood by the local community and all other stakeholders with an interest in tourism and conservation. The strategy should enable a comprehensive picture to be formed of needs and opportunities in an area, so that a range of complementary actions can be taken. One of the main benefits from working on a strategy is to provide the community with the tools and knowledge necessary for decision making. The strategy should be community-led and community-focused. However, it is essential that people with experience and knowledge of tourism and conservation are involved in its preparation.

People involved should include representatives of the local community, knowledgeable tourism operators, local entrepreneurs, relevant NGOs, conservation agencies including protected area managers, and local authorities. Links should be made as appropriate to the regional and national government level. Inputs to the strategy should include:

— careful consultation within the community covering attitudes and awareness of tourism, possible opportunities and pitfalls, existing experience, concerns and level of interest;

— a comprehensive market assessment; and

— an assessment of the natural and cultural heritage, including opportunities presented for ecotourism and sensitivities and constraints.

It is also helpful to set out a clear statement of strengths, weaknesses, opportunities and threats.The output of the strategy process should be an agreed vision for ecotourism over a specified period, together with an identification of aims, objectives and strategic priorities, an action plan, and a way of monitoring results. The action plan should identify practical initiatives, including a timescale and an indication of responsibility and resources required. It is very important, in order to avoid frustration, not to be too ambitious in terms of targets and timing.

The actions identified may include specific development or marketing projects. In some locations at least as much, or more, attention may need to be paid to action to manage tourism, including policies on development control and the handling of existing visitors. In many places, the relationship between the local community and a protected area may be an important element of the strategy, including agreed action on the level of any park admission fees and their subsequent use for conservation or within the community, which is an important issue for ecotourism.

A fundamental characteristic of community-based ecotourism is that the quality of the natural resources and cultural heritage of an area should not be damaged and, if possible, should be enhanced by tourism. Adverse impact on the natural environment should be minimised and the culture of indigenous communities should not be compromised. Ecotourism should encourage people to value their own cultural heritage. However, culture is not static and communities may wish to see change.

A practical approach is to identify the limits of acceptable change that could be brought by tourism and then to consider what level of tourism activity would generate this change. It is very important that communities decide on the level of tourism they wish to see. Consultation during the process of drawing up an ecotourism strategy should reveal the kinds of changes that might be viewed positively or negatively by local people. They can then be helped to consider what this might mean in terms of the numbers and types of visitor to look for, when they should come and their length of stay.

For example, in one community in the Amazon it was felt that more than eight visitors per month would be disruptive. Two important principles are: products developed should be based on the community's traditional knowledge, values and skills; and the community should decide which aspects of their cultural traditions they wish to share with visitors.

A similar approach can be adopted with respect to determining limits of acceptable change and of acceptable use as far as the natural environment is concerned. Here scientific knowledge may be required to enable a judgement to be made, taking account of the conditions of different sites at various times of the year. Often it is found that the quantity of visitors at any one time is a more critical factor than the overall level of visitation. Useful tools in the management of visitors include the following.

1. Agreements with tour operators over the number and size of groups to bring.

2. Codes of conducts for visitors.

3. Application of systematic environmental, social and cultural impact assessment on all proposed development. This should also be concerned with details of what is offered to visitors, such as the choice of products sold to them or the use of inappropriate sources of fuel.

4. Zoning both within and outside protected areas. This should cover both the siting of facilities and the degree of access allowed. In some locations, village communities have identified specific zones for ecotourism, both with respect to facility provision and wildlife conservation measures. A common approach is to locate tourist lodges some distance away from community villages. The planning process should ensure that monitoring measures are in place so that it is possible to tell when limits of acceptable change have been reached. Furthermore, strategies for making the necessary adjustments to overcome any problems identified will need to be established. There are many examples in the Mediterranean where environmental degradation has occurred but also places where sound planning control and community involvement have prevented over-exploitation.

Promotion of Community-based Ecotourism

The main reason why many community-based ecotourism projects have failed is that they have not attracted a sufficient number of visitors. Often, assumptions made about the marketability of a particular location or experience have been unrealistic and not based on research. As a result, promotional activity has been misdirected. A problem has been the lack of tourism knowledge not only among local communities themselves but also among advisors and supporting agencies. A thorough market assessment should be undertaken for the destination as a whole and for the individual ecotourism project. This should consider the following.

1. The patterns, profiles and interests of existing visitors to the area, based on visitor surveys. In principle, it is far easier to get more out of existing visitors than to attract new ones.

2. The location of the area with respect to established tourist circuits in the country. Proximity to these and opportunities for deflection make a considerable difference.

3. The level, nature and performance of existing ecotourism products which are competitors but also potential collaborators.

4. The activities of inbound tour operators and ground handling agents in the country and coverage by international tour operators.

5. Existing information and promotional mechanisms in the area.

The unique or particular qualities that an area might offer in comparison to other existing products should be identified. From knowledge of the market, an initial profile of target visitors should be drawn up. Attention needs to be paid to the different opportunities and requirements of experienced ecotourists, more general mid-market visitors who enjoy seeing nature and local culture, backpackers, and educational markets. In some areas, the domestic visitor market may offer more potential than international travellers. The level and nature of marketing should also take into account the environmental and cultural integrity of the area and implications for visitor numbers.

A marketing plan should be prepared for all projects, which relates market research to a promotional programme. A vital ingredient for many projects is to form a close working relationship with one or more specialist tour operators. These should be selected carefully to ensure they are well established and are delivering reliable business. Contact, directly or through handling agents, should be made in the early stages, before the development of the offer has occurred, so that the operator can advise on what can be sold and adjustments, if necessary, can be made.

Setting up a fully saleable programme can take time. An initial step may be to test market the programme with one or two groups. This also has the advantage of acquainting the community with the experience of handling guests.

Quality of Products

Quality is about delivering an experience that meets or exceeds visitor expectations. These, in turn, will vary according to the type of visitor coming, which reinforces the need for effective market research. Although luxury and sophistication may not be sought, an important section of the ecotourism market, often handled by tour operators, is looking for a rich wildlife experience, comfortable and reliable accommodation and efficient business handling. It can sometimes be difficult for communities to deliver this. On the other hand, the special sense of discovery, welcome and privilege which a community visit can provide is something valued by many visitors. There are three key requirements.

1. Attention to detail, ensuring that what is offered, at whatever level, is well delivered.

2. Quality and accuracy of promotion and information, giving reassurance but also ensuring that expectations match reality. All visitors in this market are increasingly looking for a high level of information provision.

3. Authenticity and ambience. Ecotourists respond to genuine and traditional values and experiences and they do not want this to be manufactured for them. Some issues relate to specific components of the offer.

    1. The quality of the wildlife and landscapes, in terms of relative uniqueness, attractiveness and abundance. If this is high, a project has a greater chance of success. Without it, the quality of the associated facilities and derived experiences becomes more important.

    2. The mix of natural and cultural experiences. Many visitors are looking for a combination.

    3. *Accommodation*: cleanliness is of primary importance, but issues such as ablution and toilet arrangements, general functionality, privacy and overall design and ambience can be significant. Different requirements in terms of investment and sophistication exist between lodges and camping grounds.

    4. *Guiding and interpretation*: a fine balance between local colour and story telling, and scientific knowledge and accuracy is often sought. This may require involvement of different people, including an opportunity for local people to be trained as guides and interpreters.

    5. *Local produce and handicrafts*: although visitors may look for authenticity, it is very important to avoid the depletion of cultural artefacts and other resources. Quality products can be made and sold which reflect an area's traditions and creativity without devaluing them.

    6. *General experience of village life, including folklore*: this can prove an experience highly valued by visitors. It can provide an incentive to keep local culture and pass on local knowledge.

7. *Participation*: some visitors value the opportunity to participate in activities. Conservation participation programmes are a specific sub-sector of ecotourism and can be community-based.

Linkages between projects, with different locations providing different elements, according to availability and aptitude. This can also lead to savings on certain costs, including marketing. Sometimes communities work in conjunction with other organisations such as park authorities. Irrespective of the type of product on offer, each component should be the subject of a carefully prepared business plan. This should develop the market assessment and marketing approach, cover practical details of delivery, address personnel and responsibilities, and include a full costing and risk assessment.

Managing Impacts

In some communities, useful income has been earned through, for example, the supply of thatching. Often it can be better to use existing buildings rather than engaging in new development, and this should be considered first. Action should be taken, both at the development stage and in operating facilities, to reduce consumption of water and energy, reduce waste and avoid pollution. Low energy technologies appropriate to the location should be applied where possible. Recycling should be encouraged and all forms of waste disposal should be carefully managed, with a principle of taking as much waste away from the site as possible. Use of environmentally friendly transport should be positively favoured, both in the planning of programmes and in the information supplied.

In order to minimise economic leakage, every effort should be made to use local produce and services, and to favour the employment of local people. This may require action to identify local, sustainable sources. Producers can be assisted through the formation of local groups and networks, and help with contacts, marketing and pricing. Local communities should be encouraged and helped to take account of these issues themselves without any effect on their living standards, through information, training and demonstration. Feedback to them from visitors will help. Influencing the actions taken by visitors and tour operators is very important.

Some elements of good practice can be included as firm requirements in contracts with the private sector. A number of national and international tourism certification schemes provide formal recognition of good practice in managing impacts on the environment and local communities. In selecting a scheme, the criteria it uses should be carefully considered. In particular, certification should be based on action taken rather than simply expressed intention.

Support

Many of the issues raised in these guidelines point to the importance of capacity building and training programmes with local communities. It is important to get the level of delivery and content right. This should be carefully discussed with the communities themselves. In general, it has been found that short, technical courses have had little impact. A useful way of generating ideas, giving confidence and putting across knowledge is through contacting, visiting or meeting other projects which are already experienced in community-based ecotourism. There are various examples where this has been particularly successful. Most projects require some form of financial support. However, the nature of the financial assistance must avoid inhibiting incentive and causing problems within and between communities. Soft loans and long-term credit, well targeted to local needs, may be most appropriate.

The use of local committees to approve financial offers has proved successful in some areas. It is important to demonstrate to governments and donor agencies the success of small community-based projects, including appropriate credit schemes, in order to encourage more financial assistance programmes. As well as technical marketing advice, projects can be assisted through access to national research data, help with visitor surveys, and linkages to marketing outlets such as national tourist board promotions and websites. The establishment of registers of community-based ecotourism projects, if possible backed by efficient reservation systems, should be encouraged.

A very valuable way of providing technical support is through establishing networks between projects. Some countries have associations of communitybased tourism initiatives. These not only raise awareness and provide marketing support but can also promote common quality standards, deliver training and financial assistance and generally represent the sector in the commercial and political arena.

Significant additional benefits can be achieved through improving communication with visitors themselves and with the tour operators who bring them. These benefits include greater awareness of environmental and social issues, modifying behaviour when visiting, and generating direct-support for local communities and conservation causes.

'In almost all cases, the experience of a community-based tourism programme will have an impact on how people think in future about the area and habitats they have visited. However, this can be made more or less meaningful depending on the information they receive before, during and after the visit, and how it is delivered. Careful attention should be paid to the messages put out by tour operators to their clients and to the quality of guiding and interpretation on site. Mechanisms for follow-up contact should be explored. Visitors should be encouraged to 'multiply' their experience by writing and talking about it.

A number of codes of conduct for visitors have been produced. Some are generic, others are area or site specific. These tend to cover questions such as prior reading and understanding, selection of operators and destinations, respect for local cultures, minimising environmental impact, purchasing decisions, activities to avoid, and conservation issues to support. Similarly, codes for tour operators cover issues such as particular environmental and cultural issues in the destination concerned, selection of sites, relationship with indigenous communities, messages to put across to staff and clients, and more specific instructions and regulations. These codes can be adapted for all ecotourism destinations.

CHAPTER 6

PLANNING AND DEVELOPMENT OF ECOTOURISM

Ecotourism is a concept that evolved over the last 20 years as the conservation community, people living in and around protected areas, and the travel industry witnessed a boom in nature tourism and realised their mutual interests in directing its growth. Ecotourism has brought the promise of achieving conservation goals, improving the well-being of local communities and generating new business - promising a rare winwin-win situation. Relations among conservationists, communities and tourism practitioners have not always been smooth and collaborative. However, the concept and practice of ecotourism brings these different actors together.

Ecotourism has emerged as a platform to establish partnerships and to jointly guide the path of tourists seeking to experience and learn about natural areas and diverse cultures. Specific circumstances on all sides motivated this new interest in ecotourism. On the conservation side, protected area managers were in the midst of redefining conservation strategies. For practical reasons, they were learning to combine conservation activities with economic development as it became obvious that traditional conservation approaches of strict protectionism were no longer adequate and new ways of accomplishing goals were needed. For years, conservationists established and managed protected areas through minimal collaboration with the people living in or near these areas. Circumstances in many countries, particularly in developing regions, have changed dramatically in recent years and have affected approaches to conservation.

The rationale behind ecotourism is that local tourism businesses would not destroy natural resources but would instead support their protection. Ecotourism would offer a viable strategy to simultaneously make money and conserve resources. Ecotourism could be considered a "sustainable" activity, one that does not diminish natural resources being used while at the same time generating income.

The explosion in nature tourism has lead to the need to address the impacts of the industry. The growing demand for nature-based tourism sparked interest among protected area managers to place tourism within a conservation context. Travelers have been the driving forces in the evolution of ecotourism. Ecotravellers - conscious and sensitive nature tourists - constitute a growing segment of the nature tourism market that seeks sensitive interaction with host communities in a way that contributes to sustainable local development. Local communities meanwhile increasingly expect to play a role in the management of tourism.

As a popular word, ecotourism has been used loosely. But if implemented fully, it is a critically important conservation strategy for achieving sustainable development. There are a variety of related terms that are frequently linked, and sometimes confused with ecotourism, including the following: Nature tourism is simply tourism based on visitation to natural areas. Nature tourism is closely related to ecotourism but does not necessarily involve conservation or sustainability. This is the type of tourism that currently exists in most natural areas before a plan is established and conservation measures are in place. As different elements of ecotourism are integrated into a nature tourism programme, its effect on the environment may change.

Sustainable nature tourism is very close to ecotourism but does not meet all the criteria of true ecotourism. For example, a cable car carrying visitors through the rainforest canopy may generate benefits for conservation and educate visitors, but because it represents a high degree of mechanisation and consequently creates a barrier between the visitor and the natural environment, it would be inappropriate to describe as an ecotourism initiative. In altered and heavily-visited areas, sustainable nature tourism may be an appropriate activity.

A huge range of players with varying interests and goals participates in ecotourism. Some play more prominent roles than others, but almost all are represented in the development and management of ecotourism sites. A key to the success of ecotourism is the formation of strong partnerships so that the multiple goals of conservation and equitable development can be met. Partnerships may be difficult because of the number of players involved and their different needs, but forging relationships is essential. The key players can be classified as: protected area personnel, community organisations and individuals, private sector tourism industry members and a variety of government officials and nongovernmental organisations. Their effective interaction creates effective ecotourism.

Ecotourism, then, is a multifaceted, multidisciplinary, multi-actor activity requiring communication and collaboration among a diverse range of actors with different needs and interests. Consequently, achieving ecotourism is a challenging process though ultimately enormously rewarding for all involved.

ECOTOURISM IN PROTECTED AREAS

Ecotourism attractions, whether they are wildlife viewing possibilities or dramatic natural landscapes, tend to be found in these protected natural areas. Protected areas began evolving in the 19th century largely as a response to these pressures. By "protected area" we mean a piece of land or body of water, which is characterised by the following:

a) The area has defined borders.

b) The area is managed and protected by an identifiable entity or individual, usually a government agency. Increasingly, though, governments are delegating responsibility for protected areas to other entities that are private, public or a combination thereof.

c) The area has established conservation objectives that its management pursues.

The rapid increase in the numbers and territorial coverage of protected areas since the 1960s coincides with more rapid increases in the aforementioned pressures. Traditionally, protected areas are set aside and managed by government authorities in order to protect endangered species or examples of outstanding scenic beauty. In much of the southern hemisphere, financial pressures on government budgets, global trends towards decentralisation and a society which increasingly values the role of nongovernmental participation have caused some profound changes in the way protected areas are being administered and managed. These changes are manifested in two major ways:

a) Protected areas are increasingly expected to generate some portion of the funding necessary for their own management.

b) Many other organisations, both private and public, are becoming involved in the management and conservation of protected areas, either in partnership with the traditional government agencies in charge of protected areas or by managing their own protected areas.

An additional responsibility of park managers is to bring conservation to the people. Without a constituency for conservation, we will ultimately fail. This constituency can be local, national and international. Ecotourism is crucial for achieving this goal and not just as a source of conservation finance. The link between ecotourism and protected areas is therefore inevitable and profound.

Tourism and ecotourism are usually a part of the management strategy for a protected area. The degree to which tourism activities are pursued depends upon the priority assigned to them by the area managers, who in turn should be guided by a planning document prepared for that purpose. The planning document should be the result of a comprehensive evaluation of the area's natural and cultural resource base. It determines the stresses, their sources and the real threats to the area's natural and cultural integrity, as well as the strategies to reduce these threats.

The plan should define the area's long-term management objectives and a zoning scheme that identifies where certain activities may take place. What we have is a coming together of two different forces to create a symbiotic relationship: ecotourism needs protected areas, and protected areas need ecotourism. Ecotourism is increasingly being considered as a management strategy for protected areas that, if implemented appropriately, constitutes an ideal sustainable activity. It is designed to:

a) have minimum impact upon the ecosystem;

b) contribute economically to local communities;

c) be respectful of local cultures;

d) be developed using participatory processes which involve all stakeholders; and

e) be monitored in order to detect negative and positive impacts.

There are many compelling reasons why conservationists and protected area managers are considering ecotourism as a protected area management tool. These include the following:

— Conventional tourism sometimes appears as a source of stress on the biodiversity of a protected area. In other cases, ecotourism can be regarded as an appropriate strategy for addressing threats to conservation targets. Nature tourists are presently going to protected areas in growing numbers. At a minimum, managers must control tourism's negative impacts. Even if elaborate visitor centers and extensive tourism businesses are not created, measures must be taken to ensure that these growing numbers of visitors do not negatively impact the biodiversity values of a protected area. These measures include increasing staff, developing monitoring systems and refining environmental education efforts. Managing visitors and minimising impacts is a primary responsibility of protected area managers.

— Ecotourism can capture economic benefits for protected areas. Visitors with no place to spend money are missed opportunities. Hundreds of thousands of dollars of potential revenue currently are being lost both to protected area managers and local communities because tourists do not have adequate opportunities to pay fees and buy goods and services.

— Properly implemented, ecotourism can become an important force for improving relations between local communities and protected area administrations. This relationship is perhaps the most difficult aspect of ecotourism since it involves levels of communication and trust between different cultures and perspectives that have traditionally been difficult to achieve.

— Ecotourism can provide a better option than other competing economic activities for natural areas. Many natural areas are threatened and need to be fortified in order to survive; ecotourism may help guard against some of these threats and competing land uses. For example, a successful ecotourism programme can forestall implementation of logging in an area by generating greater revenues, especially over the long term.

— By implementing ecotourism in protected areas, we are demonstrating that tourism need not be massive and destructive.

Tourism presents a mix of opportunities and threats for protected areas. Ecotourism seeks to increase opportunities and to reduce threats. If an opportunity is realised, then it becomes a benefit. If a threat is not avoided, then it becomes a cost. There are no automatic benefits associated with ecotourism; success depends on good planning and management. Carelessly planned or poorly implemented ecotourism projects can easily become conventional tourism projects with all of the associated negative impacts. Opportunities and threats, and consequently benefits and costs, will vary from situation to situation, from group to group and from individual to individual within groups.

Benefits to one group may be costs to another. Determining which opportunities to pursue and which threats to abate is a subjective decision that can best be made by involving all stakeholders. Ranking the importance of each benefit is part of the compromising involved in the ecotourism planning process. The entire spectrum of ecotourism's opportunities and threats does not apply to every protected area. For example, in a protected area that attracts primarily domestic visitors, opportunities to generate foreign exchange are limited, but good opportunities may exist to raise conservation awareness locally. Environmental degradation will vary depending on the fragility of natural resources and the types of activities that are permitted. The circumstances of each protected area create a particular set of opportunities and threats.

Bringing money into protected areas is a major concern of conservationists. Governmental funds available for protected areas have been decreasing globally, and many important natural areas will not survive without new sources of revenue. Tourism offers opportunities to generate revenue in diverse ways, such as entrance fees, user fees, concessions to the private sector and donations. New funds allow protected area managers to handle tourists better and to hold the line against other threats.

Entrance or visitor use fees are charged directly to visitors to see and experience an area. Collected at the gate, entrance fees have various structures. In some cases, a flat fee is charged. In other cases, multi-fee systems are established with various rates for different types of users. Typically, foreign tourists are charged more than local visitors are. User fees are charged for specific activities or for using special equipment in a protected area, such as electrical hook-ups when camping or various rental fees.

Private sector concessions include snack bars, restaurants, lodges, gift shops, canoe rentals and tour guides. All of these can be privately owned or managed with a portion of the profits returned to the protected area. This arrangement is favorable because it reduces business responsibilities assigned to untrained or uninterested protected area personnel. Concessions allow protected areas to benefit from the energy and profits of private sector enterprises. However, concessions must be negotiated for the protected area's long-term benefit and must be monitored closely. This monitoring ensures, for example, that the concessionaire is complying with contracted services such as trash removal, trail maintenance, etc.

Protected areas with threatened or unique plants and animals can request financial assistance for them. Visitors who have just completed a fascinating nature experience are a perfect audience for this type of appeal. Many protected areas report a high rate of success with setting up donation programmes for specific campaigns. There may be other ways tourism can bring revenue to protected areas. For example, visitors may also be "virtual," which entails visiting a web site that has been established for a protected area.

Donations may also be solicited from a much larger audience of such virtual visitors. For some protected areas, tourism can become the primary revenue generator. For others, it will be only one of many sources of financial contributions. But for almost all protected areas, visitors should be considered a readily available and accessible income source that should be exploited equitably for long-term sustainability and to promote return visits.

New jobs are often cited as the biggest gain from tourism. Protected areas may hire new guides, guards, researchers or managers to meet increased ecotourism demands. In surrounding communities, residents may become employed as taxi drivers, tour guides, lodge owners or handicraft makers, or they may participate in other tourism enterprises. In addition, other types of employment may be augmented indirectly through tourism. More bricklayers may be needed for construction. More vegetables may be needed at new restaurants. More cloth may be needed to make souvenirs. Many employment sources are enhanced as tourism grows.

In some cases, community residents are good candidates for tourism jobs because they know the local environment well. Residents are ideal sources of information; for example, they can tell visitors why certain plants flower at particular times and what animals are attracted to them. As indigenous residents of the area, community members have much to offer in ecotourism jobs. However, care must be taken to protect the rights (sometimes referred to as intellectual property rights) of local peoples so that their knowledge is not exploited or appropriated unfairly by visitors or a tourism programme.

We should not overstate the value of ecotourism employment in rural areas. There are a few important caveats to consider. First, while there is often talk of big tourism dollars, ecotourism will generally not be an economic bonanza for an entire community. More realistically, it will generate some jobs, depending on how popular the protected area is, but will not automatically become an income provider for hundreds of people. Furthermore, many ecotourism jobs will be part time and seasonal and should be considered only supplemental to other sources of income.

Overall, ecotourism employment will likely be limited for most communities. A second concern about ecotourism employment is the nature of jobs for communities. Typically, few management and ownership positions are available. Tourism will always have many service positions, because it is a labor-intensive industry. But communities may resent ecotourism if their members are not represented in the higher levels of employment. The profitability of tourism for local residents is minimised if they are offered only menial jobs and not given opportunities for advancement.

Additionally, gender inequities may be generated while the higher paying guiding and management jobs all go to men and women are restricted to lower paying laundry, cleaning and cooking positions. Another hurdle to ecotourism employment is the issue of training. For many residents, new employment is a major personal and professional transition. It sounds good on paper that former loggers may become tour guides, thereby conserving the trees they used to cut. But redirecting careers is a big undertaking.

New job candidates need information on all facets of ecotourism management. They need training in business development as well as such basics as languages, food preparation, first aid, motorboat maintenance, interpretation, group management, etc. They need access to international markets. New tourism jobs require new skills and therefore training. Ecotourism project plans need to budget for these training costs over the long term. In addition, there are many social and cultural considerations in switching jobs; it involves lifestyle changes.

Visitors, or the potential to attract visitors, are among the reasons that government officials and residents support protected areas. For government officials, declaring areas protected and providing the financial assistance to maintain them is often a difficult process. These officials face many competing interests in making decisions about how to use land and marine resources.

Conserving protected areas requires long-term vision; this is often a challenge for government officials, especially when confronted with the prospect of short-term financial gains for logging, mining and agriculture activities. But as government officials review land and water-use options, nature tourism may sway them to provide protected status to an area or strengthen the protective status of an existing protected area or reserve, particularly if it can generate income and provide other national benefits.

International tourism motivates government officials to think more about the importance of managing natural areas. Visitors are more likely to visit and support a natural area if it is protected, which in turn adds justification to the existence of protected areas. Visitation to the area may be the impetus for residents near protected areas, or potential protected areas, to support the continued protection of these areas.

Tourists visiting nature sites boost economies at the local, regional and national levels. If tourism brings jobs to residents at the local level, they then have more money to spend locally, and economic activity within the area increases. The same pattern may occur at the regional and national levels. Nature tourists arrive in the capital city of a country. They may stay for a few days or travel to the countryside. Along the way they use hotels, restaurants, shops, guide services and transportation systems.

Typically, a multitude of businesses benefit directly from nature tourists. Although these businesses usually are set up to accommodate the broader groups of international and national tourists, nature tourists are an added market. Also, some operations whisk visitors directly from the airport to a full itinerary in a private protected area, thus leaving the visitor no opportunity to spend money in local communities. In such cases, it is important to ensure that there are mechanisms such as airport taxes to obtain at least some tourist revenue. Industries that support tourism, such as manufacturing and farming, are also affected by numbers of tourists. Growing ecotourism creates a stronger economy throughout the country.

ECOTOURISM MANAGEMENT PLAN (EMP)

Six principal management strategies that form the backbone of an Ecotourism Management Plan (EMP). These strategies ensure that tourism activities contribute to the conservation goals of a protected area. However, most of them also have application for ecotourism development in any context, including in those areas that are not formally protected. Alternatively, the General Management Planning process may have emphasized the need for establishing discrete visitor use zones or establishing mechanisms for generating income from tourism for site management. To ensure that tourism at a protected area is sustainable, it is necessary to implement a strong and effective management programme that involves all stakeholders in dynamic, creative ways. Figure 1 illustrates how diverse ecotourism management strategies contribute to an ecotourism management plan.

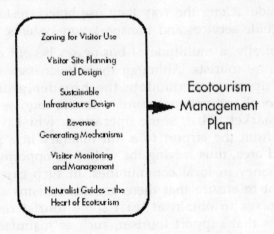

Figure 1. Ecotourism management strategies

Zoning for Visitor Use

The appropriate zoning of an ecotourism site is

fundamental to all other management strategies. Zoning is the division of a site into a number of different sectors, or zones, for the purpose of distributing different types of use or non-use (i.e., protection) in the most appropriate places. The number and types of zones depend upon:

a) the management objectives and priorities of the site;

b) the quality and variety of the natural and cultural resources and the degree of alteration they have suffered; and

c) the types of use that have been planned.

Each zone is managed to maintain or achieve a particular natural setting within which ecotourism and other activities take place, and thus, each zone has its own set of rules and regulations for activities carried out within its boundaries. Typically, a site or a protected area within it, has one or two zones dedicated primarily for public use (such as ecotourism) and two or three other zones where public use is of secondary consideration.

The appropriate zoning of a protected area is fundamental to all other management strategies. Zoning is a mechanism for assigning overall management objectives and priorities to different areas (zones) within the site or protected area. By assigning objectives and priorities to these zones, planners are also defining what uses will and will not be allowed. These parameters are usually based upon the characteristics of the natural and cultural resource base, the protected area objectives and political considerations. The decision to guide public use using ecotourism principles is a type of political decision that affects zoning. Managers guide their day-to-day decisions about the area's operations based in part upon the zoning structure.

The initial zoning for a protected area is usually determined in the General Management Plan (GMP). However, although ecotourism may be identified in the

GMP as the desired public use, current information may be insufficient to define where public use zones should be located. The zoning system will determine the natural conditions for which the different sectors of an area will be managed. Some zones may be managed to maintain a very fragile ecosystem where even highly managed, low volume visitation may not be an option.

However, well-managed ecotourism activities provide managers with more options, and thus ecotourism might be permitted in some zones where conventional tourism would not be. Generally speaking, most protected areas provide for two or more types of public use zones. Intensive Use Zones are where most of the high impact, concentrated visitor use takes place, and Extensive Use Zones are where more low impact, generally trail-oriented visitor use occurs. Other zones usually set aside parts of the protected area as "untouchable" zones where very little or no public use occurs, either due to remoteness or resource fragility.

Intensive Use Zones are usually quite small in area, representing less than one percent of a protected area's territory. Extensive Use Zones are generally larger but still represent only a minor part of the site's overall territory. Other zones may permit some ecotourism activities on a highly limited and controlled basis, frequently requiring a permit.

Ecotourism encompasses a large number of potential activities ranging from ecolodges to trekking. While planning for an ecotourism site, you should decide toward what part of the ecotourism market you wish to orient the site's activities. The wide spectrum of potential ecotourists includes some who will arrive with full understanding of what it means to be ecologically sensitive, while others will need to be educated on site. "High-end" visitors will expect fairly comfortable facilities, while more adventurous or lower spending visitors will seek or settle for more basic facilities.

The type of visitor you wish to have at your site can determine the types of ecotourism activities you plan for as well as the degree to which they are developed. Traditionally, most protected area administrators have opted to manage for a wide variety of visitors, although the facilities they provide generally are geared towards the more basic visitor demands, e.g., campgrounds, trails, small-scale food service. High-end visitors usually find lodging and food service outside the protected area.

As a general rule, high-end visitors spend more money but also require more and better quality facilities that have the potential for causing more environmental impact. The lower-end visitor spends less money but requires only basic services and infrastructure. The more adventurous and lower-end visitor is more likely to utilise sections of the protected area/ecotourism site that are distant and relatively undeveloped.

If ecotourism is to be fully implemented, protected area managers must ensure that tourism activities are low impact and extremely well managed. If these conditions are met, then ecotourism significantly widens the scope and locations for public-use activities. High-end visitor infrastructure may need to be located in a separate zone to avoid possible conflicting uses. Planners and managers must balance the need to generate income with the potential negative impacts and positive economic and educational impacts that can occur with ecotourism.

When determining zones, one should take into consideration their unique biophysical, social and administrative/ management factors. It is a management principle that use in zones not managed for specific attributes will gravitate toward busy, more-developed settings with easier access and a high density of people with corresponding increased evidence of human activity. A well-planned zoning system improves the quality of the visitor experience and provides more options that can enable tour operators to adapt to market changes. The natural resources of a zone should be described in terms of their sensitivity and ecological importance. The abundance and density of unique, endangered, endemic or charismatic species that may be important for the zone should be noted.

Visitor Site Planning and Design

Most ecotourism sites and protected areas are fairly large covering thousands or tens of thousands of hectares. When planning for ecotourism on a large tract of land or water, visitor use is generally concentrated in a few small sites where most infrastructure is located. Generally referred to as visitor sites, where most visitor use occurs, they are also where some very serious impacts may occur, which is why they must be planned in. Usually visitor site planning takes place within the context of the preparation of an Ecotourism Management Plan (EMP) and after a zoning scheme for an area has been established.

Site plans are prepared as part of the EMP or as a subsequent step when more time and funding are available. Visitor site designation is the result of the EMP process, which analyses natural and cultural resources and attractions of the protected area, makes a determination about the area's ecotourism potential and then selects certain strategic sites for ecotourism concentration based on their:

— inclusion of current and potential ecotourism attractions;

— accessibility;

— potential to concentrate visitor use with a minimum of impact; and/or

— history of previous use. In most cases, it is advisable to use sites that have already received some human intervention in order to avoid impacting intact sites.

The EMP should also make recommendations about the type(s) of infrastructure for the site without being specific about exact locations. The site planning process determines exact locations of infrastructure, taking into account the site's ecological sensitivity and positioning the infrastructure from a visitor management perspective (e.g., location of trails in relation to a campground or attraction). A financial feasibility study will determine whether there is or will be sufficient demand for a business-focused infrastructure and an environmental feasibility study will assess its environmental viability.

The visitor site planning process is best carried out by a team made up of a landscape architect, a biologist or ecologist, and an environmental engineer, who should all have some training in environmental impact evaluation and tourism infrastructure. It is advisable to include a local resident on the team who is familiar with the site and/or environmental conditions in the area.

When determining exactly where buildings and infrastructure should be located, planners should take into consideration the following:

a) General Considerations:

— Ecosystem maintenance should take precedence over development considerations.

— Plan landscape development according to the surrounding context rather than by overlaying familiar, traditional patterns and solutions.

— Maintain both ecological integrity and economic viability, as both are important factors for a sustainable development process.

— Allow simplicity of functions to prevail while respecting basic human needs of comfort and safety.

— Maximise/minimise exposure to wind through plan orientation and configuration, number and position of wall and roof openings, and relationship to grade and vegetation.

— Recognise that there is no such thing as waste, only resources out of place.

— Assess feasibility of development in long-term social and environmental costs, not just short-term construction costs.

— Plan to implement development in phases to allow for the monitoring of cumulative environmental impacts and the consequent adjustments for the next phase.

b) Specific Considerations:

— *Capacity*: As difficult as it may be to determine, every site has a limit for development and human activity. A detailed site analysis should determine this limit based on the sensitivity of the site's resources, the ability of the land to regenerate and the mitigating factors incorporated into the site's design. The determined limits of acceptable change also depend upon the sensitivity that planners have for the site's environment, and the adaptations that are made to mitigate construction and operational impacts.

— *Density*: Siting of facilities should carefully weigh the relative merits of concentration versus dispersal of visitor use. Natural landscape values may be easier to maintain if facilities are carefully dispersed. Conversely, concentration of structures leaves more undisturbed natural areas.

— *Slopes*: Steep slopes predominate in many park and recreational environments. Siting infrastructure on slopes can cause erosion problems and should be avoided.

— *Vegetation*: It is important to retain as much existing native vegetation as possible to secure the integrity of the site. Natural vegetation is an essential aspect of the visitor experience and should be preserved. Use native species for land generation, and avoid the use of exotic plant species. Minimise, or even eliminate, the use of lawns. In areas such as the tropics, most nutrients are held in the forest canopy, not in the soil; loss of trees can therefore causes nutrient loss. Shorelines and beachfronts should not be intensively developed or cleared of vegetation.

— *Wildlife*: Avoid the disruption of movement, nesting patterns, feeding and roosting sites of threatened, endangered or focal wildlife species by sensitive siting of development and by limits set on construction activity and facility operation. Allow opportunities for visitors to be aware of indigenous wildlife (observe but not disturb). Also, be aware that in some ecosystems, particularly on islands, tourism activities can lead to the introduction of invasive species.

— *Views*: Views are critical and reinforce a visitor's experience. Site design should maximise views of natural features and minimise views of visitor and support facilities. To do so, avoid high structures. Buildings should remain below tree/ horizon line and be invisible from the air and on ground arrival as much as possible. Colours used on exteriors should blend, not contrast, with the natural environment.

— *Natural Hazards*: Development should be located with consideration of natural hazards such as precipitous slopes, dangerous animals and plants, and hazardous water areas.

— *Energy and Utilities*: Conventional energy and utility systems are often minimal or nonexistent in potential ecotourism sites. Siting should consider possible connections to off-site utilities or, more likely, spatial needs for on-site utilities.

b) Infrastructure should be placed to take advantage of natural ventilation possibilities when consistent with esthetic and other considerations.

c) Environmentally appropriate technologies and facilities for the treatment of organic wastes should be considered, such as composting, septic tanks and biogas tanks.

d) Provision should be made for ecotourism appropriate facilities that may not have been considered in the original site planning recommendations: facilities for trash storage until removal from the site, solar panels or other appropriate energy source, maintenance buildings and sites for treatment of gray water.

e) Water sources should be located where other activities will not impact them and in such a manner that water use will not significantly alter existing watercourses. Waterlines should be located to minimise disruption of earth and adjacent to trails wherever possible.

— *Visitor Circulation Systems*: Infrastructure elements such as lodging and trails should be located to optimise visitor circulation: minimum distances, minimum disturbance to natural features, easily located by visitors, etc. Trails should be designed with environmental and cultural interpretation in mind and with attractions and sensitivity the primary determining factors in placement. Wherever possible, trails should be offered for differing levels of physical ability and should form a closed loop to avoid visitors retracing their steps, thus improving their experience.

— *Conflicting Uses*: If the site provides for different types of visitor use, for example ecolodge and campground, make sure these uses are sufficiently separated geographically so that they do not conflict. Safety, visual quality, noise and odor are all factors that need to be considered when siting support services and facilities. These areas need to be separated from public use and circulation areas. Under some circumstances, utilities, energy systems and waste recycling areas can be a positive, educational part of the ecotourism experience. Siting should be compatible with traditional agricultural, fishing and hunting activities. Some forms of development that supplant traditional land uses may not be responsive to the local economy.

— *Impact Monitoring*: Specific indicators and standards should be established to monitor the impact of the site's use as an ecotourism location.

Sustainable Infrastructure Design

Sustainability does not require a diminished quality of life, but it does require a change in mindset and values toward a less consumptive lifestyle. These changes must embrace global interdependence, environmental stewardship, social responsibility and economic viability. Sustainable design must use an approach to traditional design that incorporates these changes in mindset. This alternative design approach recognises the impacts of every design choice on the natural and cultural resources of the local, regional and global environments. Some guiding principles of sustainability include:

— Recognise interdependence. The elements of human design interact with and depend on the natural world, with broad and diverse implications at every scale. Expand design considerations to recognise even possible distant effects.

— Accept responsibility for the consequences of design decisions - upon the well-being of humans, the viability of natural systems, and their right to co-exist.

— Eliminate the concept of waste. Evaluate and optimise the full life cycle of products and processes to approach the state of natural systems in which there is no waste.

— Rely on natural energy flows. Human designs should, like the living world, derive their creative forces from perpetual solar income. Incorporate this energy efficiently and safely for responsible use.

— Understand the limitations of design. No human creation lasts forever and design does not solve all problems. Treat nature as a model and mentor, not an inconvenience to be evaded or controlled.

Sustainable design balances human needs (rather than human wants) with the capacity of the natural and cultural environments. It minimises environmental impacts and the importation of goods and energy, as well as the generation of waste. Any development would ideally be constructed from natural sustainable materials collected on site, generate its own energy from renewable sources such as solar or wind, and manage its own waste.

Sustainable building design must seek to:

— Use the building (or non-building) as an educational tool to demonstrate the importance of the environment in sustaining human life.

— Reconnect humans with their environment for the spiritual, emotional and therapeutic benefits that nature provides.

— Promote new human values and lifestyles to achieve a more harmonious relationship with local, regional and global resources and environments.

— Increase public awareness about appropriate technologies and the cradle-to-grave energy and waste implications of various building and consumer materials.

— Nurture living cultures to perpetuate indigenous responsiveness to, and harmony with, local environmental factors.

— Relay cultural and historical understanding of the site with local, regional and global relationships.

Managing natural factors

Sustainable design seeks harmony with its environment. To properly balance human needs with environmental opportunities and liabilities requires detailed analysis of the specific site. How facilities relate to their context should be obvious so as to provide environmental education for its users. Although the following information is fairly general, it serves as a checklist of basic considerations to address once specific site data are obtained.

Climate

— apply natural conditioning techniques to effect appropriate comfort levels for human activities; do not isolate human needs from the environment

— avoid overdependence on mechanical systems to alter the climate

— analyse whether the climate is comfortable, too cold or too hot for the anticipated activities, and then decide on mitigation of the primary climatic components of temperature, sun, wind and moisture that can make the comfort level better.

Temperature

— temperature is a liability in climates where it is consistently too hot or too cold

— areas that are very dry or at high elevation typically have the characteristic of large temperature swings from daytime heating to nighttime cooling, which can be flattened through heavy/massive construction to yield relatively constant indoor temperatures

— when temperature is predominantly too hot for comfort:

  a) minimise solid enclosure and thermal mass

  b) maximise roof ventilation

  c) use elongated or segmented floor plans to minimise internal heat gain and maximise exposure for ventilation

  d) separate rooms and functions with covered breezeways to maximise wall shading and induce ventilation

  e) isolate heat generating functions such as laundry and kitchens from living areas

  f) provide shaded, outdoor living areas such as porches and decks

  g) capitalise on nighttime temperatures, breezes or ground temperatures

— when climate is predominantly too cold for comfort:

  a) consolidate functions into the most compact configuration

  b) insulate thoroughly to minimise heat loss

  c) minimise air infiltration with barrier sheeting, weather-stripping, sealants and airlock entries

  d) minimise entries not oriented towards sun exposure.

Sun

— sun can be a significant liability in hot climates but is rarely a liability in cold climates

— sun can be an asset in cool and cold climates to provide passive heating

— design must reflect seasonal variations in solar intensity, incidence angle, cloud cover and storm influences

— when solar gain causes conditions too hot for comfort:

  a) use overhangs to shade walls and openings

  b) use site features and vegetation to provide shading to walls with eastern and western exposure

  c) use shading devices such as louvers, covered porches and trellises with natural vines to block sun without blocking out breezes and natural light

  d) orient broad building surfaces away from the hot late-day western sun

  e) use light-coloured wall and roofing materials to reflect solar radiation

  f) in tropical climates use shutters and screens, avoiding glass and exposures to direct sunlight

— when solar gain is to be used to offset conditions that are too cold for comfort

  a) maximise building exposure and openings facing south (facing north in the southern hemisphere)

  b) increase thermal mass and envelope insulation

  c) use dark-coloured building exteriors to absorb solar radiation and promote heat gain.

Wind

— wind is a liability in cold climates because it strips heat away quicker than normal; wind can also be a liability to comfort in hot dry climates when it causes the human body to dehydrate and then overheat

— wind can be an asset in hot, humid climates to provide natural ventilation

    a) use natural ventilation wherever feasible; limit air conditioning to areas requiring special humidity or temperature control such as artifact storage and computer rooms;

    b) use wind scoops, thermal chimneys or wind turbines to induce ventilation on sites with limited wind.

Moisture

— moisture can be a liability if it is in the form of humidity, causing such stickiness that one cannot cool evaporatively (cool by perspiring)

    a) strategies to reduce the discomfort of high humidity include maximising ventilation, inducing air flow around facilities and venting or moving moistureproducing functions such as kitchens and shower rooms to outside areas

— moisture can be an asset by evaporating in hot, dry climates to cool and humidify the air

    a) techniques for evaporative cooling include placing facilities where breezes will pass over water features before reaching the facility and providing fountains, pools and plants.

Other climatic considerations

— rainfall can be a liability if any concentrated runoff from developed surfaces is not managed to avoid erosion

— rainfall can be an asset if it is collected off roofs for use as drinking water

— storms/hurricanes/monsoons/typhoons

    a) provide or make arrangements for emergency storm shelters

b) avoid development in flood plain or storm surge areas

c) consider wind effects on walls and roofs when designing structures

d) provide storm shutters for openings

e) design facilities to be light enough and of readily available and renewable materials to be safely and economically sacrificed to large storms, or of sufficient mass and detail to prevent loss of life and material.

Topography

— consider building/land interfaces to minimise disturbance to site character, skyline, vegetation, hydrology and soils

— consolidate functions or segment facilities to reduce footprint of individual structures to allow sensitive placement within existing landforms

— use landforms and the sensitive arrangement of buildings to:

a) help diminish the visual impact of facilities enhance visual quality by creating a rhythm of open spaces and framed views

b) orient visitors to building entrances

c) accentuate key landmarks, vistas and facilities.

Water bodies

— capture views and consider advantages/ disadvantages of offshore breezes

— safeguard water from pollutants from the development itself and from the users

— minimise visual impact of development on waterfront zones

    a) use building setbacks

    b) consider building orientation and materials

    c) avoid light pollution

— allow precipitation to naturally recharge groundwater wherever possible.

Pests

— design facilities to minimise intrusion by noxious insects, reptiles and rodents

— ensure that facility operators use natural means for pest control.

Cultural resources

— archeological and other sites of cultural importance should be respected and not negatively impacted

— understand the local culture and the need to avoid the introduction of socially unacceptable or morally offensive practices

— consult with local indigenous population for design input as well as to foster a sense of ownership and acceptance

— include local construction techniques, materials and cultural considerations in the development of new facilities

— incorporate local expressions of art, handiwork, detailing and, when appropriate, technology into new facility design and interior design.

Sensory experience

    a) Visual

        — provide visitors with ready access to educational materials and experiences to enhance their understanding and appreciation of the local environment and the threats to it

- incorporate views of natural and cultural resources into routine activities to provide opportunities for contemplation, relaxation and appreciation
- provide visual surprises within the design of facilities to stimulate the educational experience.

b) Sound

- locate service and maintenance functions away from public areas
- space lodging units and interpretive stops so that natural and not human sounds dominate
- restrict the use or audio level of unnatural sounds such as radios and televisions.

c) Smell

- allow natural fragrances of vegetation to be enjoyed
- direct air exhausted from utility areas away from public areas.

Management of Energy Consumption

An ecotourism site has a responsibility to use the most advanced techniques possible to reduce energy consumption, utilise local renewable sources of energy and educate visitors about environmentally responsible energy consumption. Just as a site has primary natural and cultural resources, it has primary renewable energy resources, such as sun, wind and biogas conversion. Solar applications range from hot water preheating to electric power production with photovoltaic cells. Windpowered generators can provide electricity and pumping applications in some areas.

The biogas conversion process reduces gas or electricity costs and eliminates the release of wastewater effluent into water resources. Biogas can be used for water heating, cooking and refrigeration. The availability, potential and feasibility of primary renewable energy resources must be analysed early in the planning process as part of a comprehensive energy plan. The plan must justify energy demand and supply and assess the actual costs and benefits to the local, regional and global environments. Certainly it is best to avoid adding to pressure on the natural environment by avoiding the use of polluting fossil fuels such as diesel and oil.

Water supply

Sustainable design should respect the water resources with diligence whatever the natural distribution. The challenge of sustainable design applies more to areas where fresh water is not limited than to dry areas where the economics of high-cost water tends to promote wise stewardship. The principles of sustainable design apply without reservation to all types of climates. In a park or ecotourism development, where health considerations are paramount, water issues center on providing safe drinking, washing, cooking and toilet-flushing water.

Pay close attention to issues of water supply and sustainability, impact of use on local communities and sensible economies (e.g., baths vs. showers). The cornerstone of any domestic water supply programme is conservation. Water conservation includes using water of lower quality such as reclaimed wastewater effluent, gray water or runoff from ground surfaces for toilet flushing or irrigation of the landscape or food crops. These uses do not require the quality of water that is needed for internal consumption, bathing or washing. With the proper type of wastewater treatment and plumbing hardware, sea water can be used as a toilet-flushing medium.

User education and awareness are key to successful water conservation. Visitors should receive interpretation about the source of the water and the types of energy required to process and distribute water at the site. Positive reinforcement should be provided to visitors by informing them of their actual water savings as well as their responsibility in achieving the goal of water conservation. Appropriate signs of high quality material should be put in restrooms to indicate that management places a high priority on water conservation and to confirm goals and expected bnehaviours of visitors.

Waste Management

Preventing pollution in a sensitive setting means thinking through all of the activities and services associated with the facility and planning them in a way that they generate less waste. Waste prevention leads to thinking about materials in terms of reduce, reuse and recycle. The best way to prevent pollution is not to use materials that become waste problems. When such materials must be used, they should be reused onsite. Materials that cannot be directly reused should be recycled.

Solid Waste: Convert biodegradable waste to compost that can be used on site or made available to local food producers. Non-biodegradable wastes should be separated on site and transported to a properly managed site for adequate disposal. This may have the additional benefit of creating additional employment and could provide environmental education and improve local community infrastructure. Use biodegradable detergents, fats, guest soaps and shampoos, etc. Limit the use of disposable plastic containers, utensils and wrappings and advise guests in advance of ecolodge policy.

Sewage: Evaluate the relative impacts and merits of dry toilets, anaerobic bioseptic treatment (and biogas production), aerobic bioseptic treatment and constructed wetlands. Wastewater should be treated to a level acceptable for agriculture and released into an irrigation system for a small garden behind the facility. This accomplishes three goals at once: use of wastewater instead of simply releasing it into the watershed, reduction of local food resources consumption and provision of fresh, organic produce.

Waste prevention requires training the operators, including all users of the system, and performing diligent maintenance. Most waste problems are created by lack of attention. Because waste prevention represents a change in the way activities are carried out, it requires an extra effort to ensure that these practices are maintained until they become routine. In situations with high turnover of both employees and visitors, continuous training and education will be essential.

Pollution prevention

Avoid the use of aerosols (housekeeping sprays, etc.) - use more economical and eco-friendly "hand-pumped" materials, which must be biodegradable. Swimming pool backwashes should have chemical removing filters, and consider alternatives to chlorine for pool cleaning. All gasoline and oil tanks should be secured in their own reservoirs to avoid leakage into the surrounding environment, and vehicles' used oils should be collected and shipped out. Minimise light pollution, especially artificial lighting in outdoor areas, to avoid disturbance to wildlife and to keep the stars visible from the lodge.

Monitoring of Visitor Impact

Every time a visitor sets foot in an ecotourism site, he/ she causes a negative impact. This is an unavoidable fact. An ecotourism programme initiates many public use activities that will have impacts, both positive and negative. An Ecotourism Management Plan seeks to minimise the negative impacts and ensure that they are outweighed by positive ones. The monitoring and managing of visitor impacts are fundamental ecotourism management strategies but ones that are frequently left unattended. If you do not know what effects your ecotourism activities are having on the site's natural environment and the surrounding communities, then you cannot say that you are successful. Careful monitoring of impacts, both positive and negative, needs to be a primary activity of the site's overall management. Monitoring costs money and requires trained personnel and the assistance of interested stakeholders.

The first methods developed to address tourism impacts evolved from the concept of carrying capacity, which originated in the field of range management. Several definitions of carrying capacity have been offered in the literature depending on how and where the concept was applied. Initially, it was used only to indicate how much tourism activity was too much. Researchers began to realise that looking only at numbers of visitors was not sufficient. They demonstrated that what visitors did, when they did it and a number of other circumstances were frequently more important in determining visitor impacts than simply the number of visitors.

The degree of impact depends upon many variables in addition to the amount of use: the degree of site hardening; the motivations and bnehaviours of visitors; the mode of visitor transport and lodging; the effectiveness of guides; and the season(s) in which most use occurs. Therefore, when managers use the term "carrying capacity" they usually are referring to this more broadly-defined meaning: the amount and type of use that an area can sustain before impacts become unacceptable.

The more simple and straightforward concept of carrying capacity-limiting numbers of visitors-can sometimes be used as a solution for mitigating impacts in restricted, small-scale situations, but not usually on a protected area basis or large ecotourism site situation. There are two very good methodologies that can be used to monitor visitor impacts: "Measures of Success" and "Limits of Acceptable Change."

Limits of Acce ptable Change (LAC) has evolved specifically to allow tourism to address the shortcomings of the carrying capacity concept, although it has been applied to more general management situations. Measures of Success can be applied to any management planning situation, not just ecotourism, and relies primarily upon the setting of objectives that can be easily monitored. In order to measure the effectiveness of ecotourism as a conservation strategy, the biodiversity health of the protected area needs to be monitored.

Naturalist Guides

Naturalist guides play a central role in the implementation of the ecotourism concept. They are the principal providers of the educational element to the ecotourism activity, and their capacity and commitment ensures that the negative impacts of tourism are minimised. At the same time, guiding is an obvious economic opportunity for people from local communities. These and other important benefits underline the importance of a protected area establishing and implementing a naturalist guide training and licensing programme.

The use of tour guides in protected areas is not a new phenomenon. Guides have been a part of nature tourism in many places for many years. These tour guides usually were employed by private tour operators and had little or no relationship to the protected area they worked in. Over the years, this situation began to change as protected area managers realised the potential for using guides to increase contact with visitors and for accomplishing other ecotourism objectives as well.

Naturalist guides truly play a multifaceted role. They have responsibilities to their tour operator employers, to their clients the visitors, and to the protected areas and communities where they work. Tour operators count on guides to provide experience-enriching interpretation of natural and cultural attractions to add value to the tourists' itinerary. They also require guides to manage logistical aspects of trips in the field, such as coordinating with accommodation, food and transport service providers. Guides are responsible for the tourists' safety and in general represent their tour operator employer in the field.

Tourists look to the naturalist guide for information, interpretation and insight about the places they are visiting; for help preparing for a visit through formal briefings and informal talks; and generally to be a friendly, knowledgeable intermediary with unfamiliar places and people. Protected area authorities look to the guides as extensions of the park ranger staff, to educate the visitors, to protect the natural and cultural resources of the area visited, to participate in monitoring programmes and generally to support the conservation objectives of an area. In addition to these roles, a naturalist guide should seek to inspire visitors to become supporters of conservation.

Environmental interpretation is a subset of communication that focuses on how best to explain environmental/ ecological concepts to the general public. One of the central tenets of ecotourism is to educate the visitor. Naturalist guides, who spend a considerable amount of time with visitors, are in a perfect position to educate through skilled interpretation. Many local residents have a detailed knowledge of the plant and animal life as well as of other natural and cultural attractions. They can also relate first-hand experiences with wildlife, medicinal plants and other local phenomena.

As the main contacts that visitors may have with an ecotourism site, guides serve as important role models both to visitors and their own communities. Their attitude and bnehaviour send an important message to others about the ecotourism concept. Does the guide pick up pieces of trash along the hiking trail? Does the guide actively support and cooperate with site managers by reporting illegal activities? Does the guide adapt ecotourism to his/her own home and community situation? Some tour guides make a point of discussing the importance of conserving the incredible diversity found at a site, what the major threats to it are and what visitors might do to help conserve it.

Unfortunately, not all visitors to ecotourism sites know how to behave appropriately in sensitive natural and cultural settings. It is the guides' responsibility to ensure that visitors are aware of all applicable rules and regulations as well as other relevant ethical considerations. In a polite but firm manner, they must make sure that visitors comply with whatever restrictions there may be. This is perhaps the most difficult role that guides have because their major responsibility is to help provide visitors with an enjoyable experience. As members of the private sector, it can, in rare situations, create a conflict of interest between the guides' conservation obligations and their obligation to the visitor and, in some cases, their employer.

For example, a tour operator might promise clients a close encounter with a whale, but a guide may judge that at a given moment the whales seen in the distance are nursing young and should not be approached. The guide's obligations to an employer and to a park authority might be divergent at this point. Guides need special training in how best to deal with these situations. They also must be vested with the authority to report and ⁻leal with infractions of rules and regulations.

Since guides visit the ecotourism site/protected area on a frequent basis, they are in a unique position to notice certain kinds of impact, such as trail erosion, increasing rareness of a particular bird species, etc. They are also in an excellent position to carry out formal monitoring observations for the site's managers. In many places, guides take the time to carry out observations of the number of nesting birds or of the regeneration of a plant species in a designated quadrant. This can be of valuable assistance to a site's managers when they are short-handed or simply do not have trained personnel to carry out these tasks.

When guides are from local communities, they can serve an important role in improving communication between the site's administration and local people. This is particularly important when there may be some misunderstanding between the two different "communities," which there frequently is. Naturalist guides in the Galapagos Islands and other places have established their own organisations to further conservation objectives. In the Galapagos Islands, they have been especially helpful in obtaining local support for the Park Service in the face of illegal fishing activities originating outside the islands.

In order for a naturalist guide system to work well in an ecotourism site situation, several conditions must be met. The site must have effective control over the use of guides and the conditions under which guides will operate with in the site. This implies that managers either own the site or that there is legislation or some other legal mandate for exercising this control. Most effective guide systems have a licensing mechanism.

The site's administration, or some higher authority acting at the administration's request, will issue a license to guide visitors within the site if the guide complies with relevant rules and regulations. The site's administration reserves the right to suspend or revoke the license if a guide's bnehaviour is inappropriate. Licenses are usually extended to those individuals who pass a training course or a test.

The site's administration reserves the right to set other criteria for attending a training course, such as: being a member of a local community, being of a minimum age, the absence of a police record and having a minimum level of education. It is important to avoid flooding the market with too many licensed guides as this would force down wage levels as many compete for an insufficient number of jobs. However, it is necessary to have a sufficient number of guides to satisfy demand; a rough guide would be to license about 25% more guides than will be working each season.

In spite of the control that the site's administration must exercise over the guides' activities, the relationship between them should be more than one of employer and employee. Both the site administration and the guide have much to offer each other, and they should actively carry out their respective roles in order to benefit from each other's work. Unfortunately, it is not uncommon for one side or the other to lose sight of their mutually supportive roles and for the relationship to become non-productive. Constant and positive feedback is the best way to avoid this situation. Involving tour operators and guides in the ecotourism programme planning process from the beginning is also crucial.

Ecotourism encourages the inclusion of local people in as many circumstances as possible. While it may be useful to utilise local people as naturalist guides, managers should realise that residents may not be "natural" naturalist guides. Their interests or educational levels may be obstacles to reaching the level of expertise required of guides at a site. Significant training may be needed before they can function effectively.

Work availability is a very sensitive issue in many situations. Naturalist guides have the potential to earn significantly more money than other members of their community. For this reason, when a site initiates a naturalist guide system, there are sometimes many more candidates than available work. Managers must be careful not to create high expectations among guide candidates, especially if visitor numbers are not sufficient to guarantee work for everyone. If some candidates for a training course are selected over others who appear to have similar qualifications, conflicts may arise. Site managers may do several things to minimise these problems:

— Ensure that specific criteria are used to select guide candidates and that the criteria are strictly followed.

— Limit training course size to a specific number of people and accept candidates on a first come, first serve basis.

— Initiate policies that encourage or mandate the use of local guides in the ecotourism site or in specific locations or zones within the site. This may cause conflicts with other, non-local guides.

— Encourage the creation of a naturalist guides association that will help to organise guides and their response to a limited number of guiding opportunities, e.g., a system of rotation. This is also an excellent way to minimise cutthroat competition and to standardise prices. The site could mandate that guides charge only a certain amount for a given service, but the mandate would be better received and complied with if the guides were allowed to determine their own price structure.

CHAPTER 7

DEVELOPING SUSTAINABLE TOUR OPERATION

Tourism in today's world finds it necessary to manipulate and modify the environment to suit its purpose. Tourism certainly can contribute to environmental degradation and be self-destructive; it also has potential to bring about significant enhancement of the environment. With tourism-induced change, an Important issue, for example, is irreversibility, which in part is a function of the resilience of the resource base, along with the spatial and temporal pattern of impacts, and the scope for compensatory managerial response.

An influential conference held in Canada on 'Global opportunities for business and the environment' concluded that sustainable development holds considerable promise as a vehicle for addressing the problems of modern tourism. Clearly, what seems to be occur ring is recognition of the interdependence between environmental and economic issues and policies, and ultimately, acceptance of the notion that sound environmental management in tourism does not merely cost, it pays. Of course, convincing decision makers of the good sense, both environmentally and commercially, of the merits of a sustainable approach to tourism may not be easy. It can be difficult to demonstrate conclusively the costs over time of environmental degradation, especially when set against the more immediate returns forgone by adopting a more restrained pattern of development.

The tourism industry of the 1990s is showing commendable preparedness to apply the principles of best practice environmental management to its activities, especially at the largerscale, corporate level. If the process of achieving sustainable forms of development in a growing tourism industry is a formidable challenge, the task takes on additional dimensions when set against the many forces for change facing the industry as it moves into the next century. New spatial forms and settings must be anticipated as tourist developers seek to service a diverse and expanding array of interests and opportunities. Tourism can be a very volatile industry, sensitive to changes in perception and taste, and to altered biophysical, economic or political circumstances. Thus the theme of change is constant on the tourism scene. In a business sense, the professional component of tourism is constrained to keep abreast of change, and be aware of, and respond to changes in travel preferences, in technology, and in the many factors which help fashion 19 the travel market. A danger is that in these circumstances, sustainability may only be pursued in a financial or business management context.

Ecologically sustainable tourism development may be seen as too expensive and irrelevant to business success. Much research interest focuses on the responses of tourists and tourism to changing socioeconomic circumstances, to political., cultural and attitudinal changes to improvements in spatial awareness and communication, and to growing environmental concern for sustainability. In almost five decades since the resurgence of organized travel in 1948, tourism, as an international phenomenon, has passed through different stages until it has become a gigantic instrument in the develop mental strategy of a good number of countries.

As expressed by the World Tourism Organisation, tourism is ambivalent. It can contribute positively to socioeconomic and cultural achievements, while at the same time it may cause the degradation of environment and the loss of local identity. It should therefore be approached with a global methodology. It is incumbent upon the destination to orient its tourism growth towards meeting its socioeconomic objectives and environmental requirements. Moreover, tourism growth must coincide with the destination's prevailing value system and cultural integrity, and satisfy the needs of its local population.

The term sustainability, which has gained prominence in tourism jargon, is seen by many writers as an important part of the philosophy permeating all levels of tourism policy issues and practice from national to local. Others understand sustainability as a deep-rooted concept that relates to the fundamentals of life which sometimes are obscured by the ongoing public/private debate, regulation and rationalized government intervention. Needless to say sustainable development and management of tourism resources should coincide with economic, sociocultural, health, safety and environmental objectives at national, regional and local levels.

Tourism's multifaceted function, as a socioeconomic and politico-cultural phenomenon, as a complex industry, and as a profession having its own rules and code of ethics, requires a broad intellectual background and specialized education and/or training to enable its policy makers and professionals to keep abreast of the scientific and technological changes. If we just think of the various organizational, marketing planning and technical aspects of tourism, we must realize how complex round tourism development is. The old classical approach to tourism ⸱⸱blem-solving through day-to-day tactics can no longer hold good in the face of a rapidly growing and swiftly changing world tourism industry.

While tourism has become increasingly appreciated as a contributor to he national economics of some leading tourist destinations, lack of sufficient information about the scope and essence of that activity as well as of the processes linked to it are still widespread. It is important, however, to ask what alternative forms of tourism prove to be sustainable and which do not. Some forms of tourism are considered by some writers as sustainable, such as ecotourism and special interest tourism, although as yet no empirical research has proved such claims.The crucial question in this connection is whether tourism sustainability, at least within the narrow confines of some alternative tourism forms, could be a reality. The answer to the above question is positive. Yes, tourism sustainability could be a reality. It is the by-product of a multitude of factors that contribute to the successful present integration and future continuity of tourism it the macro and micro levels in destinations.

As all socioeconomic, vultural, political and environmental factors and subject to change in time and space, sustainability is therefore a relative term and not an absolute fact. Markets, fashions, tastes, motivations, images, trends and destinations are all likely to change, at least in the long term. Thus tourism has to be humane and adaptive to the needs of the tourists, responsive to the needs of local communities, socioeconomically and culturally well planned, and environmentally sound. The difficulty is to determine how tourism can protect and enhance opportunities for future generations of tourists and host communities while change continues to prevail. This is the challenge that tourism sustainability has to face and surmount. Such challenge manifests itself in evolving tourist behavioural patterns and forms, progress in host community attitudes towards tourism, and change in technology and marketing opportunities. Tourism must offer products that are operated in harmony with the local environment, community attitudes and cultures, so that these become the permanent beneficiaries and not the victims of tourism development.

INTERNATIONAL GUIDELINES FOR SUSTAINABLE TOURISM

The International Guidelines for activities related to sustainable tourism development are intended to assist Parties to the Convention on Biological Diversity, public authorities and stakeholders at all levels, to apply the provisions of the Convention to the sustainable development and management of tourism activities. They will provide technical guidance to policy makers, decision makers and managers with responsibilities covering tourism and/or biodiversity, whether in national or local government, the private sector, indigenous and local communities, non governmental organizations or other organizations, on ways of working together with key stakeholders involved in tourism and biodiversity in order to contribute, inter alia, to functioning ecosystems; sustainable tourism in functioning ecosystems; fair and equitable sharing of benefits; information and capacity-building; restoration of past damage.

While the guidelines were developed focusing on vulnerable terrestrial, marine and coastal ecosystems and habitats of major importance for biological diversity and protected areas, they are appropriate for tourism and biological diversity in all areas. Governments, international institutions and development agencies should take these guidelines into account in their policies, programmes and activities, and support their implementation, especially in developing countries and should encourage the exchange of experiences and lessons learned concerning their implementation.

A Broad Scope

The guidelines cover all forms and activities of tourism, which should all come under the framework of sustainable development, in all geographic regions. These include, but are not limited to, conventional mass tourism, ecotourism, nature- and culture-based tourism, cruise tourism, leisure and sports tourism.

Management

Management should be based on a consultative process involving multi-stakeholder participation. The management process needs to be undertaken through a multi-stakeholder process. Governments will normally coordinate this process at national level. This process may also be undertaken at more local levels and at community level. It is important for Governments to consult with and involve all relevant stakeholders ensuring strong involvement of indigenous and local communities throughout the management process, including decision-making on use of biodiversity resources.

Interdepartmental and inter-organizational structures and processes should be established to ensure coordination to guide policy development and implementation and to improve awareness and exchange of knowledge among stakeholders at all levels. A consultative process, based on multi-stakeholder participation, should be established to ensure ongoing and effective dialogue and information sharing and the stakeholder engagement and participation in the whole process. The establishment of partnerships should be encouraged.

Ten steps for management

The management process comprises ten steps for management of sustainable tourism and biodiversity:

1.   Baseline information and review;

2.   Vision and goals;

3.   Objectives;

4.   Review of legislation and control measures;

5.   Impact assessment;

6.   Impact management;

7.   Decision making;

8.   Implementation;

9.   Monitoring;

10. Adaptive management.

Baseline information and review

Baseline information enables informed decision making and impact assessment. Its compilation should follow the ecosystem approach. For tourism and biodiversity, the baseline information could include information at national and local levels on current economic, social and environmental conditions, considering also the structure and trends within the tourism sector and an account of benefits from, and costs of, tourism to local communities. Information on damage done to the environment in the past, environmental and biodiversity resources, including any special features and sites of particular importance and culturally sensitive areas could also be provided in this phase of the process. National biodiversity strategies, action plans and reports and national, subnational and local sustainable-development plans are also a good source of baseline information.

Information for consideration as part of baseline information includes traditional knowledge as well as scientific information. All relevant stakeholders may contribute information to this process, including biodiversity managers and indigenous and local communities. Collation and synthesis of information provided will need to be undertaken by an appropriately qualified team, drawing on a range of expertise. Together with the Government which typically assumes the responsibility of the exercise, all stakeholders should be involved in review of the collated baseline information available, and in the synthesis of this information.

The baseline information gathering and review process should make full use of the clearing-house mechanism under the Convention on Biological Diversity, as well as of relevant networks such as the World Network of Biosphere Reserves, World Heritage sites and Ramsar sites.

Vision and goals

An overall vision and goals is important for the effective management of tourism and biodiversity, and for ensuring that it contributes to poverty alleviation.

The vision and goals take into account national and regional sustainable development plans for economic and social development and for land-use, as well as the baseline information and review. The main vision and goals are established to seek to maximize the positive benefits of tourism on biodiversity, ecosystems, and economic and social development, while minimizing negative social and environmental impacts from tourism. They can cover economic and planning matters (i.e. sharing of benefits, integration and diversification of activities, zoning and control of development), ecological and scientific matters (i.e. function of ecosystems, biodiversity conservation and sustainable use), social concerns (i.e. poverty alleviation, protection of indigenous resources, participation and involvement of indigenous and local communities), and dissemination of information and capacity building.

The vision and goals will form the basis of national strategies or master plans for sustainable development of tourism in relation to biodiversity, and vice versa. Governments should take into account local and community level visions and goals when preparing the national level visions and goals.

Objectives

The objectives focus on actions to implement the overall vision and goals. The objectives may include clear targets, a timetable for their achievement and details of areas where tourism development and activities are potential development options, including details of the type and scale of such development and activities that would be acceptable and impact management measures that would be appropriate.

Governments should provide national planning frameworks and planning guidance to ensure that developments or activities are not undertaken outside areas set out in the objectives. Previous to any developments, analysis of market conditions and trends should be carried out to check the viability of the market.

Governments may also wish to consider measures to establish and support conservation areas, by:

(a) ensuring appropriate legal recognition to designated areas;

(b) establishing reserves based on the biosphere reserve concept;

(c) strengthening the protected area network;

(d) using economic policy tools and encouraging the private sector to actively support conservation efforts.

Review of legislation and control measures

Legislation and appropriate regulatory mechanisms and tools are essential for the effective implementation of any overall vision, goals, and objectives.

A review of legislation and control measures (such as land-use planning, environmental assessment, building regulations and standards for tourism) may be necessary to update and further develop legislation and control measures. Such a review could include provisions for increasing indigenous and local communities land-management, access and ownership, decision-making on issues related to tourism development, and activities and for increasing collective rights.

Legislation and control measures considered could include approval and licensing for tourism development and activities, incentives for sustainable tourism and the application of economic instruments for the management of tourism and biodiversity. The control of the planning and siting of tourism facilities and the establishment of infrastructures could also be considered and addressed by the legislation. In this context, integrated land use management and environmental assessment could be used to develop policies and measure their impacts.

Impact assessment

Impact assessment includes assessment of the environmental, social, cultural, economic effects, both positive and negative, of proposed developments.

Governments are encouraged to develop mechanisms for impact assessment with the participation of all stakeholders, including nature conservation bodies, and to ensure effective implementation of existing mechanisms. Comprehensive impact assessments are important for all tourism developments and activities, and should take into account cumulative effects from multiple development activities of all types at all levels. Governments, through appropriately qualified teams, will normally undertake evaluations of the adequacy of impact assessments submitted by proposers of tourism developments or activities. If the information provided is not sufficient, or the impact assessment inadequate, then further impact assessment studies may need to be undertaken.

Indigenous and local communities concerned should be fully involved in impact assessment, which should also recognize the contribution of traditional knowledge in the development, implementation and review of appropriate and effective methodologies and criteria to be used for impact assessment.

Impacts of tourism in relation to the environment and biological diversity may include analysis of land-use, consumption and depletion of local natural resources, considering damages and alterations to habitats and ecosystems. Impact assessment could also consider contamination and pollution from different sources due to tourism activities, deterioration of resources, production of waste and the introduction of alien species and pathogens. Socio-economic and cultural impacts on different segments of the population should also be considered, including social degradation of local communities, impact on traditional practices and lifestyles, incomes and jobs.

The potential benefits of tourism may include the creation of revenues for the maintenance of natural areas and contribution to economic development, through the creation of new infrastructures and services, jobs and the provision of funds, as well as the through the diversification of the economy.

Impact management

Impact management is essential to avoid or minimize any potential damage to biodiversity conservation and sustainable use that tourism development or activities might cause. To be sustainable, tourism should be managed within the carrying capacity and limits of acceptable change for ecosystem and sites, and to ensure that tourism activities contribute to the conservation of biodiversity. Tourism should be restricted, and where necessary prevented, in ecologically sensitive areas.

Proposals for tourism development or activities may incorporate proposals for impact management. Impact management can include measures for the siting of tourism development and activities and measures to control tourist flows in and around tourist destinations and key sites, to promote appropriate behavior by tourists so as to minimize their impacts, and to establish limits to numbers of visitors and their impacts within carrying capacity / limits to acceptable change at any site.

Impact management for tourism development and activities can include the adoption of policies, good practices and lessons learned that cover different areas of interest. The control and reduction of impact from tourist flows and activities and the minimization and prevention of pollution and waste should be addressed to minimize negative effects on destinations. The sound planning and design of facilities, services and technologies could also be addressed through the promotion of eco-efficiency, the cleaner production approach, the conservation of landscapes and natural and cultural heritages, and the preparation of contingency plans for environmental emergencies. Impact management could include policies, good practices and lessons learned on conservation and responsible use of natural resources, and considerations on local communities involvement and participation, respecting the integrity of local cultures and the use of local products and skills. Public Education and Awareness could also be included in impact management policies, for the promotion of appropriate behaviors, alignment of marketing strategies, environmental and cultural sustainability audits.

The tourism industry can assist in promoting wide implementation of management measures for sustainable tourism and the conservation and sustainable use of biodiversity in relation to tourism.

Decision making

Decision making should be a transparent and accountable process to approve or refuse a proposal, and it should always apply to the precautionary principle.

Decisions regarding tourism and biodiversity will be made concerning approval or otherwise of national strategies and plans for tourism and biodiversity, proposals for tourism development and activities and the adequacy of impact management measures in relation to anticipated impacts from tourism development and activities. Decisions will be taken ultimately by Governments (or specific authorities designated by them). Effective consultation with and participation of the communities and groups affected is an important foundation of the decision-making process. Decision makers should consider using multi-stakeholder processes as a tool for this.

Legal mechanisms should be put in place for notification and approval of tourism development proposals and for ensuring implementation of the conditions of approval of development proposals.

Decision-making should include the prior informed consent of indigenous and local communities affected by projects in order to ensure respect for the customs and traditional knowledge, innovations and practices of indigenous and local communities. Adequate funding and technical support should be provided for these groups to participate effectively.

In making a decision, conditions may be attached to any approvals that may be granted, including conditions regarding management of tourism in relation to avoidance or minimization of adverse impacts on biodiversity, and for appropriate decommissioning of tourism activities should the development cease. Decision makers may also, as appropriate, request further information from a proposer; defer a decision pending further baseline research by other agencies; or refuse a proposal.

Implementation

Implementation follows a decision to approve a particular proposal, strategy or plan, and must include implementation of all conditions that may have been set for granting of approval.

The developer and/or operator will be responsible for complying with these conditions and they can also be required to notify the designated government authority of any failures to comply with conditions attached to an approval. Any revisions or changes to an approved project, including additions and/or variations of activities, must be approved by the designated authorities. Local stakeholders should be given an ongoing opportunity to express their wishes and concerns to those managing tourism facilities and activities, based on clear, adequate and accessible information.

Governments and designated authorities will need to monitor compliance with, and enforce as necessary, conditions attached to any approval. Communities and other interested stakeholders may also monitor compliance and report their findings to the designated government authorities.

Monitoring

Monitoring and surveillance in relation to management of tourism and biodiversity includes the compliance of implementation of approved tourism developments or activities, the monitoring of the impacts of tourism activities on biodiversity and ecosystems and on surrounding population and the monitoring of general tourism activities and trends.

Developers and operators of tourism facilities and activities may be required to report periodically to designated authorities and to the public, on compliance with conditions set out in approvals, and on the condition of biodiversity and the environment in relation to the tourism facilities and activities for which they are responsible.

An inclusive monitoring and reporting system should be put in place, prior to commencement of any new tourism development or activities providing for the involvement of indigenous and local communities at all stages. Indicators to cover all aspects of management of biodiversity and sustainable tourism, including socioeconomic and cultural aspects, should be identified and selected at national and tourist destination levels.

Monitoring and surveillance in relation to biodiversity impacts should include activities undertaken to ensure respect for endangered species under relevant international agreements, prevention of introduction of alien species, compliance with national and international rules concerning access to genetic resources, and prevention of illegal and unauthorized removal of genetic resources.

Monitoring and evaluation should also include development and use of appropriate tools to monitor and evaluate tourism impacts on the economy of indigenous and local communities. Use of indicators and early warning systems should be developed as appropriate, taking into account traditional knowledge, innovation and practices of indigenous and local communities, and guidelines developed under the Convention on Biological Diversity relating to traditional knowledge.

Long-term monitoring and assessment is necessary in relation to the impacts of tourism on biodiversity, and will need to take into account the timescale for ecosystem changes to become evident. Monitoring of general environmental and biodiversity conditions and trends, as well as tourism trends and impacts, can be undertaken by governments, including designated biodiversity managers. Management measures may need to be adjusted, as appropriate, where adverse impacts on biodiversity and ecosystems are detected.

Adaptive management

Adaptive management deals with the complex and dynamic nature of ecosystems and the absence of complete knowledge or understanding of their functioning.

Ecosystem processes are often nonlinear, the outcome of such processes often shows time-lags and their level of uncertainty is increased by the interaction with social construct. Management must be adaptive in order to be able to respond to such uncertainties and contain elements of "learning-by-doing" or research feedback.

Ecosystem management must involve a learning process, which helps to adapt methodologies and practices to the ways in which these systems are being managed and monitored. Adaptive management should also take the precautionary principle fully into account. There is also a need for flexibility in policy-making and implementation. Long-term, inflexible decisions are likely to be inadequate or even destructive. Ecosystem management should be envisaged as a long-term experiment that builds on its results as it progresses.

Implementing adaptive management in relation to tourism and biodiversity will require the active cooperation and close interaction of tourism managers and biodiversity managers. Governments in conjunction with all other stakeholders and those who have management control over any specific site, will need to take actions to address any problems encountered and to keep on track towards agreed goals. Adaptive management can also be undertaken by all those who have management control over any specific site, including local government, indigenous and local communities, the private sector, non-governmental organizations and other organizations.

Notification Proccess and Information Requirements

Proposals for tourism development and activities at particular locations in relation to biodiversity, are to be submitted through the notification process.

Proposers of tourism projects, including government agencies, should provide full and timely advance notice to relevant authorities and all stakeholders who may be affected, including indigenous and local communities, of proposed developments through a formal process of prior informed approval. Considerations on the development site could include geographical description and location and its proximity to human settlements and communities and laws and regulations applicable. Economic considerations could cover the analysis of the market for proposed tourism development and activities, the description of current socioeconomic conditions and the expected changes. Ecological aspects of the site and its surroundings should include an analysis of flora, fauna and ecosystems that could be affected and the impact on local communities as well as possible transboundary effects and impacts.

Information provided should be made public, and public comment invited on all proposals for tourism development and activities.

Government response to notification of proposals for tourism development may range from approvals, with or without conditions, to refusal of the proposal. Further information from the proposer and further research by other agencies may be requested by Governments.

Publication and Awareness Raising

Public education and awareness raising campaigns need to be addressed to both the professional sectors and the general public to inform them about the impacts of tourism on biological diversity, and good practices in this area.

Public awareness campaigns will need to be tailored for various audiences, particularly stakeholders including consumers of tourism, developers and tourism operators. The private sector could play an active role encouraging conservation among clients.

Education and awareness-raising is required at all levels of government. Awareness should also be increased within and outside governments that vulnerable ecosystems and habitats are often located within lands and waters occupied or used by indigenous and local communities. It is also important to raise awareness within the academic sector responsible for training and research on issues regarding the harmonious interaction between biological diversity and sustainable tourism.

Capapcity Building

Capacity-building activities should aim to develop and strengthen the capacities of governments and all stakeholders to facilitate the effective implementation of these guidelines, and may be necessary at local, national, regional and international levels. Capacity-building activities can include strengthening human resources and institutional capacities; the transfer of know-how; the development of appropriate facilities; training in relation to biological diversity and sustainable tourism issues, and impact assessment and impact management techniques. Local communities should also be equipped with the necessary decision-making abilities, skills and knowledge in advance of future tourist in-flows, as well as with relevant capacity and training regarding tourism services and environmental protection.

Capacity-building activities should provide assistance to stakeholders in undertaking all the steps of the management processes and in strengthening mechanisms for impact assessment. Capacity-building should also include the establishment of multistakeholder processes and the training of tourism professionals.

Information exchange and collaboration regarding sustainable tourism implementation through networking and partnerships between all stakeholders affected by, or involved in tourism, including the private sector, should be encouraged.

ENVIRONMENTAL APPROACH TOWARDS TOURISM

During the 1990s, when the globalisation of tourism reached unprecedented proportions, international tourism receipts had a much higher average annual growth rate (7.3%) than that of gross world product. By 1999, international tourism receipts accounted for more than 8% of the worldwide export value of goods and services, overtaking the export value of other leading world industries such as automotive products, chemicals, and computer and office equipment. A significant proportion of world tourism expenditure takes place within industrialised countries: Europe alone accounts for around half of annual international tourism receipts. Tourism, however, is the only major service sector in which developing countries have consistently recorded trade surpluses relative to the rest of the world. Between 1980 and 1996, for instance, their travel account surplus increased from $4.6 billion to $65.9 billion, due primarily to the impressive growth of inbound tourism to countries in Africa, the Caribbean, and the Asia and Pacific regions.

The 1990s also experienced a significant growth of international tourism receipts in the 49 least developed countries: total tourism receipts in these countries more than doubled from US$ 1 billion in 1992 to over US$ 2.2 billion in 1998. Tourism is now the second largest source of foreign exchange earnings in the least developed countries (LDCs) as a whole. Tourism has also become the main source of income for an increasing number of Small Island Developing States (SIDS). Foreign exchange earnings can, however, vary significantly among these tourismdriven economies because of 'leakages' arising from imports of equipment for construction and consumer goods required by tourists, repatriation of profits earned by foreign investors and amortisation of foreign debt incurred in tourist development.

Besides export earnings, international tourism also generates an increasingly significant share of government (national and local) tax revenues throughout the world. In addition, the development of tourism as a whole is usually accompanied by considerable investments in infrastructure, such as airports, roads, water and sewerage facilities, telecommunications and other public utilities. Such infrastructural improvements not only generate benefits to tourists but can also contribute to improving the living conditions of local populations.

This increase in social overhead capital can also help attract other industries to a disadvantaged area and thus be a stimulus to regional economic development. The tourism sector is an increasingly important source of employment—including in tourism-related sectors, such as construction and agriculture—primarily for unskilled labour, migrants from poor rural areas, people who prefer to work part-time, and notably women. Because the sector is relatively labour-intensive, investments in tourism tend to generate a larger and more rapid increase in employment than equal investment in other economic activities. Furthermore, given that the sector provides a considerable amount of jobs for women and unskilled workers, tourism can significantly contribute to empowering women and alleviating poverty. At the same time, available data suggest that most workers in the tourism sector, notably in hotels and catering, tend to earn less than workers in socially comparable occupations in both developed and developing countries. In addition, the differential tends to be larger in less developed countries and regions, particularly those with high rates of unemployment amongst unskilled labour. Informal employment relations in small and medium-sized enterprises, which employ about half of the labour force in the hotel and catering sub-sectors worldwide, also contribute to a relatively high proportion of child labour and non-remunerated employment and other unacceptable forms of social exploitation in many countries.

The increasing reliance of less diversified economies on tourism also increases their vulnerability to seasonal aspects of tourism and to shocks, such as, natural disasters, regional wars and other unexpected events. The recent crisis generated by fear of international terrorism and regional conflict, for example, caused devastating immediate effects on tourism-dependent economies.

In addition, sudden changes in consumer tastes and sharp economic downturns pose significant risks to such economies, given that demand for mass tourism tends to be relatively income-elastic and can produce drastic negative responses to economic recession in source markets. Nonetheless, it is now generally recognised that tourism can make a vital contribution to employment, export receipts and national income in most countries and regions. Furthermore, tourism is often identified as the most promising driving force for the economic development of less developed countries and regions endowed with areas of natural beauty—including Small Island Developing States—because it offers them a valuable opportunity for economic diversification.

Environmental Impact of Tourism

While tourism provides considerable economic benefits for many countries, regions and communities, its rapid expansion can also be responsible for adverse environmental, as well as socio-cultural, impact. Natural resource depletion and environmental degradation associated with tourism activities pose severe problems to many tourism-rich regions. The fact that most tourists chose to maintain their relatively high patterns of consumption (and waste generation) when they reach their destinations can be a particularly serious problem for developing countries and regions without the appropriate means for protecting their natural resources and local ecosystems from the pressures of mass tourism.

The two main areas of environmental impact of tourism are: pressure on natural resources and damage to ecosystems. Furthermore, it is now widely recognised not only that uncontrolled tourism expansion is likely to lead to environmental degradation, but also that environmental degradation, in turn, poses a serious threat to tourism activities.

In addition to pressure on the availability and prices of resources consumed by local residents-such as energy, food and basic raw materials—the main natural resources at risk from tourism development are land, freshwater and marine resources. Without careful land-use planning, for instance, rapid tourism development can intensify competition for land resources with other uses and lead to rising land prices and increased pressure to build on agricultural land. Moreover, intensive tourism development can threaten natural landscapes, notably through deforestation, loss of wetlands and soil erosion. Tourism development in coastal areas—including hotel, airport and road construction—is often a matter for increasing concern worldwide as it can lead to sand mining, beach erosion and other forms of land degradation. Freshwater availability for competing agricultural, industrial, household and other uses is rapidly becoming one of the most critical natural resource issues in many countries and regions.

Rapid expansion of the tourism industry, which tends to be extremely water-intensive, can exacerbate this problem by placing considerable pressure on scarce water supply in many destinations. Water scarcity can pose a serious limitation to future tourism development in many low-lying coastal areas and small islands that have limited supplies of surface water, and whose groundwater may be contaminated by saltwater intrusion.

Over—consumption by many tourist facilities— notably large hotel resorts and golf courses—can limit current supplies available to farmers and local populations in water-scarce regions and thus lead to serious shortages and price rises. In addition, pollution of available freshwater sources, some of which may be associated with tourism-related activities, can exacerbate local shortages. Rapid expansion of coastal and ocean tourism activities, such as snorkelling, scuba diving and sport fishing, can threaten fisheries and other marine resources.

Disturbance to marine aquatic life can also be caused by the intensive use of thrill craft, such as jet skis, frequent boat tours and boat anchors. Anchor damage is now regarded as one of the most serious threats to coral reefs in the Caribbean Sea, in view of the growing number of both small boats and large cruise ships sailing in the region. Severe damage to coral reefs and other marine resources may, in turn, not only discourage further tourism and threaten the future of local tourist industries, but also damage local fisheries.

Besides the consumption of large amounts of natural resources, the tourism industry also generates considerable waste and pollution. Disposal of liquid and solid waste generated by the tourism industry has become a particular problem for many developing countries and regions that lack the capacity to treat these waste materials. Disposal of such untreated waste has, in turn, contributed to reducing the availability of natural resources, such as freshwater.

Apart from the contamination of freshwater from pollution by untreated sewage, tourist activities can also lead to land contamination from solid waste and the contamination of marine waters and coastal areas from pollution generated by hotels and marinas, as well as cruise ships. It is estimated that cruise ships in the Caribbean Sea alone produced more than 70,000 tonnes of liquid and solid waste a year during the mid-1990s.

The fast growth of the cruise sector in this and other regions around the world has exacerbated this problem in recent years. In fact, it is sometimes argued that the rapid expansion of cruise tourism calls for "the enforcement of an environmental protection 'level playing field' across the world's oceans and between the world's maritime tourism destinations".

In addition, relatively high levels of energy consumption in hotels-including energy for air-conditioning, heating and cooking—as well as fuel used by tourism-related transportation can also contribute significantly to local air pollution in many host countries and regions. Local air and noise pollution, as well as urban congestion linked to intensive tourism development, can sometimes even discourage tourists from visiting some destinations.

Uncontrolled tourism activities can also cause severe disruption of wildlife habitats and increased pressure on endangered species. Disruption of wildlife behaviour is often caused, for example, by tourist vehicles in Africa's national parks that approach wild cats and thus distract them from hunting and breeding; tour boat operators in the Caribbean Sea that feed sharks to ensure that they remain in tourist areas; and whalewatching boat crews around the world that pursue whales and dolphins and even encourage petting, which tends to alter the animals' feeding and behaviour.

Similarly, tourism can lead to the indiscriminate clearance of native vegetation for the development of new facilities, increased demand for fuelwood and even forest fires. Ecologically fragile areas, such as rain forests, wetlands and mangroves, are also threatened by intensive or irresponsible tourist activity. Moreover, as will be discussed below, it is increasingly recognised that, the rapid expansion of nature tourism (or 'ecotourism') may also pose a threat to ecologically fragile areas, including many natural world heritage sites, if not properly managed and monitored.

The delicate ecosystems of most small islands, together with their increasing reliance on tourism as a main tool of socio-economic development, means that this environmental impact can be particularly damaging since the success of the tourism sector in these islands often depends on the quality of their natural environment. In addition, pollution of coastal waters—in particular by sewage, solid waste, sediments and untreated chemicals—often leads to the deterioration of coastal ecosystems, notably coral reefs, and thus harms their value for tourism.

The equally fragile ecosystems of mountain regions are also threatened by increasing popular tourist activities such as skiing, snowboarding and trekking. One of the most serious environmental problems in mountainous developing countries without appropriate energy supply is deforestation arising from increasing consumption of fuelwood by the tourism industry. This often results not only in the destruction of local habitats and ecosystems, but also in accelerating processes of erosion and landslides.

Other major problems arising from tourist activities in mountain regions include disruption of animal migration by road and tourist facilities, sewage pollution of rivers, excessive water withdrawals from streams to supply resorts and the accumulation of solid waste on trails. In many mountain regions, small islands, coastal areas and other ecologically fragile places visited by tourists, there is an increasing concern that the negative impact of tourism on the natural environment can ultimately hurt the tourism industry itself.

In other words, the negative impact of intensive tourism activities on the environmental quality of beaches, mountains, rivers, forests and other ecosystems also compromise the viability of the tourism industry in these places. There is now plenty of evidence of the 'life-cycle' of a tourist destination, that is, the evolution from its discovery, to development and eventual decline because of over-exploitation and subsequent deterioration its key attractions. In many developing and developed countries alike, tourism destinations are becoming overdeveloped up to the point where the damage caused by environmental degradation-and the eventual loss of revenues arising from a collapse in tourism arrivals-becomes irreversible.

Examples of such exploitation of 'non-renewable tourism resources' range from a small fishing village in India's Kerala state-which saw its tourist sector collapse after two decades of fast growth, because inadequate disposal of solid waste-to several places in the industrialised world, such as Italy's Adriatic coast and Germany's Black Forest.

It can also be argued that environmental pollution and urban sprawl tend to undermine further tourist development in major urban destinations in developing countries, such as Bangkok, Cairo and Mexico City. In addition, tourism in many destinations could be particularly threatened by external environmental shocks, notably the potential threat of global warming and sea-level rise.

Significant rises in sea level could cause serious problems to tourism activities, particularly in low-lying coastal areas and small islands. Global warming is also expected to increase climate variability and to provoke changes in the frequency and intensity of extreme climate events—such as tropical windstorms and associated storm surges and coastal flooding—that may threaten tourism activities at certain destinations.

Countries and regions where the economy is driven by the tourism industry have become increasingly concerned with the environmental, as well as the socio-cultural problems associated with unsustainable tourism. As a result, there is now increasing agreement on the need to promote sustainable tourism development to minimise its environmental impact and to maximise socio-economic overall benefits at tourist destinations.

The concept of sustainable tourism, as developed by the World Tourism Organisation (WTO) in the context of the United Nations sustainable development process, refers to tourist activities "leading to management of all resources in such a way that economic, social and aesthetic needs can be fulfilled while maintaining cultural integrity, essential ecological processes, biological diversity and life support systems".

The international action plan on sustainable development agreed on at the 1992 Earth Summit in Rio de Janeiro (Brazil) —its growing economic importance, significant use of natural resources and environmental impact all contributed to its gradual introduction into the international sustainable development agenda over the past ten years. To be sustainable, tourism should be managed within the carrying capacity and limits of each ecosystem and site.

The Plan of Implementation adopted at the World Summit on Sustainable Development (WSSD), held in Johannesburg (South Africa) from 26 August to 4 September 2002, identified further measures to promote sustainable tourism development, with a view to increasing "the benefits from tourism resources for the population in host communities while maintaining the cultural and environmental integrity of the host communities and enhancing the protection of ecologically sensitive areas and natural heritages".

As similar international actions plans show, the WSSD Plan of Implementation is likely to induce States to take more progressive steps towards better governance and sustainable development. However, achieving the sustainable tourism goals contained in the WSSD Plan of Implementation will require systematic action and the availability of adequate resources at both national and international levels.

The WSSD Plan of Implementation makes particular reference to activities carried out in conjunction with the 2002 United Nations International Year of Ecotourism, amongst other international activities, in the implementation of its sustainable tourism goals. The International Year of Ecotourism offered an ideal opportunity not only to review ecotourism experiences around the world, but also to promote worldwide recognition of the important role of sustainable tourism in the broader international sustainable development agenda.

There is, however, a crucial distinction between ecotourism and sustainable tourism: while the former can be broadly defined as an alternative, nature-based type of tourism, sustainable tourism calls for adherence to the abovementioned sustainability principles in all types of tourism activities and by all segments of the tourism industry.

Ecotourism is still a relatively small segment of the overall tourism sector. At the same time, it is one of the fastest growing tourism segments and further rapid growth is expected in the future. There is, however, little agreement about its exact meaning because of the wide variety of so-called ecotourism activities provided by many different suppliers and enjoyed by an equally broad range of diverse tourists. Its main features include

— all forms of nature tourism aimed at the appreciation of both the natural world and the traditional cultures existent in natural areas,

— deliberate efforts to minimise the harmful human impact on the natural and socio-cultural environment and

— support for the protection of natural and cultural assets and the well-being of host communities.

Ecotourism can be a valuable means for promoting the socio-economic development of host communities while generating resources for the preservation of natural and cultural assets. In this way, ecologically fragile areas can be protected with the financial returns of ecotourism activities.

Ecotourism has been particularly successful in attracting private investments for the establishment of privately owned natural parks and nature reserves in an increasing number of developing countries, such as Costa Rica, Ecuador, Malaysia and South Africa. Many such reserves are well managed, self-financed and environmentally responsible, even when profit remains the main motivation behind the operation of a private reserve. In this way, the tourism industry can help to protect and even rehabilitate natural assets, and thus contribute to the preservation of biological diversity and ecological balance.

However, if not properly planned, managed and monitored, ecotourism can be distorted for purely commercial purposes and even for promoting ecologicallydamaging activities by large numbers of tourists in natural areas. Given their inadequate physical infrastructure and limited capacity to absorb mass tourism, the fragile land and ocean ecosystems of many developing countries can be literally overwhelmed by large numbers of tourists.

It is increasingly recognised, therefore, that ecotourism activities can also cause adverse ecological impact, particularly if they are not properly managed or if they involve tourist numbers beyond the local carrying capacity. Furthermore, even when ecotourism activities are carried out in a responsible manner, they tend to give priority to environmental protection, mainly by focusing on providing financial incentives for environmental conservation by local communities.

Similarly, while broader sustainable tourism strategies contain economic and social objectives, these objectives tend to be complementary to a central focus on environmental sustainability. Greater priority should thus be given to socio-economic objectives in general, and to poverty reduction in particular.

PRO-POOR TOURISM APPROACH

A pro-poor tourism (PPT) approach differs from ecotourism and other sustainable tourism strategies in that its overriding goal is to deliver net benefits to the poor. While PPT and ecotourism may have some similar objectives, the key difference is that poverty reduction is the core focus of the PPT approach, rather than a secondary component of a mainly environmental sustainability strategy.

In other words, although environmental protection remains an important PPT goal, the quality of the environment in which targeted poor groups live is only one part of a broader poverty reduction strategy. There are several reasons why tourism development could be a particularly effective tool of poverty reduction. First, as discussed earlier, tourism offers considerable employment opportunities for unskilled labour, rural to urban migrants and lower-income women. Second, there are considerable linkages with the informal sector, which could generate positive multiplier effects to poorer groups that rely on that sector for their liveli-hoods.

Third, tourism tends to be heavily based upon the preservation of natural capital—such as, wildlife and scenery—and cultural heritage, which are often "assets that some of the poor have, even if they have no financial resources". It is increasingly realised that promoting greater community participation in tourism development not only provides stronger incentives to conserve natural capital, but can also lead to a more equitable sharing of benefits and thus greater opportunities for poverty alleviation.

But while ecotourism and PPT both aim to increase community participation in general, PPT also goes beyond this goal in that it includes specific mechanisms to enhance the participation of and opportunities for the poorer segments of society. Three key components of the PPT approach are:

— improved access to the economic benefits of tourism by expanding employment and business opportunities for the poor and providing adequate training to enable them to maximise these opportunities;

— measures to deal with the social and environmental impact of tourism development, particularly the above—mentioned forms of social exploitation, as well as excessive pressure on natural resources, pollution generation and damage to ecosystems; and

— policy reform, by enhancing participation of the poor in planning, development and management of tourism activities pertinent to them, removing some of the barriers for greater participation by the poor, and encouraging partnerships between government agencies or the private sector and poor people in developing new tourism goods and services.

Some of these PPT concepts are beginning to be implemented in several developing countries, such as Ecuador, Namibia, Nepal and Uganda. In Namibia, for example, the implementation of a PPT approach to the development and management of the country's community-based tourism segment appears to have made a significant contribution towards poverty reduction.

Several studies have shown that financial returns from community-based natural resource management and tourism ventures in Namibia usually exceed their investments and are thus a viable option for generating sustainable economic returns, while promoting environmental conservation and cultural traditions in rural areas. There is now evidence of a successful introduction of the PPT approach by the Namibia Community-based Tourism Association, a non-profit organisation that supports poor local communities— including small entrepreneurs with inadequate skills or access to financial resources—in their efforts to develop tourism enterprises in the country. Its members at both micro and macro levels, mainly through the provision of grants, loans, training, capacity building in the areas of institutional development and marketing training, as well as in negotiations with relevant government agencies and the mainstream tourist industry.

UNEP PRINCIPLES ON THE IMPLEMENTATION OF SUSTAINABLE TOURISM

The principles cover:

1. Integration of Tourism into Overall Policy for Sustainable Development

2. Development of Sustainable Tourism

3. Management of Tourism

4. Conditions for Success

Integration of Tourism into Overall Policy for Sustainable Development

a. National Strategies

b. Interagency Coordination and Cooperation

c. Integrated Management

d. Reconciling Conflicting Resource Uses

National Strategies: Ensure that tourism is balanced with broader economic, social and environmental objectives at national and local level by setting out a national tourism strategy that is based on knowledge of environmental and biodiversity resources, and is integrated with national and regional sustainable development plans.

— Establish a national tourism strategy that is updated periodically and a master plan for tourism development and management.

— Integrate conservation of environmental and biodiversity resources into all such strategies and plans.

— Enhance prospects for economic development and employment while maintaining protection of the environment.

— Provide support through policy development and commitment to promote sustainability in tourism and related activities.

Interagency Coordination and Cooperation: Improve the management and development of tourism by ensuring coordination and cooperation between the different agencies, authorities and organisations concerned at all levels, and that their jurisdictions and responsibilities are clearly defined and complement each other.

— Strengthen the coordination of tourism policy, planning development and management at both national and local levels.

— Strengthen the role of local authorities in the management and control of tourism, including providing capacity development for this.

— Ensure that all stakeholders, including government agencies and local planning authorities, are involved in the development and implementation of tourism.

— Maintain a balance with other economic activities and natural resource uses in the area, and take into account all environmental costs and benefits.

Integrated Management: Coordinate the allocation of land uses, and regulate inappropriate activities that damage ecosystems, by strengthening or developing integrated policies and management covering all activities, including Integrated Coastal Zone Management and adoption of an ecosystem approach.

— Maximise economic, social and environmental benefits from tourism and minimise its adverse effects, through effective coordination and management of development

— Adopt integrated management approaches that cover all economic activities in an area, including tourism.

— Use integrated management approaches to carry out restoration programmes effectively in areas that have been damaged or degraded by past activities.

Reconciling Conflicting Resource Uses: Identify and resolve potential or actual conflicts between tourism and other activities over resource use at an early stage. Involve all relevant stakeholders in the development of sound management plans, and provide the organisation, facilities and enforcement capacity required for effective implementation of those management plans.

— Enable different stakeholders in the tourism industry and local communities, organisations and institutions to work alongside each other

— Focus on ways in which different interests can complement each other within a balanced programme for sustainable development.

Development of Sustainable Tourism

The role of planning

a. Planning for Development & Land-use at sub-National Level

b. Environmental Impact Assessment (EIA)

c. Planning Measures

Planning for Development & Land-use at sub-National Level: Conserve the environment, maintain the quality of the visitor experience, and provide benefits for local communities by ensuring that tourism planning is undertaken as part of overall development plans for any area, and that plans for the short-, medium-, and long-term encompass these objectives.

— Incorporate tourism planning with planning for all sectors and development objectives to ensure that the needs of all areas are addressed. (Tourism planning should not be undertaken in isolation.)

— Ensure that plans create and share employment opportunities with local communities.

— Ensure that plans contain a set of development guidelines for the sustainable use of natural resources and land.

— Prevent ad hoc or speculative developments.

— Promote development of a diverse tourism base that is well-integrated with other local economic activities.

— Protect important habitats and conserve biodiversity in accordance with the Convention on Biological Diversity.

Environmental Impact Assessment (EIA): Anticipate environmental impacts by undertaking comprehensive EIAs for all tourism development programmes taking into account cumulative effects from multiple development activities of all types.

— Examine impacts at the regional national and local levels.

— Adopt or amend legislation to ensure that EIAs and the planning process take account of regional factors, if necessary.

— Ensure that project proposals respond to regional development plans and guidelines for sustainable development.

Planning Measures: Ensure that tourism development remains within national and local plans for both tourism and for other types of activity by implementing effective carrying capacity programmes, planning controls and management.

— Introduce measures to control and monitor tour operators, tourism facilities, and tourists in any area.

— Apply economic instruments, such as user fees or bonds.

— Zone of land and marine as an appropriate mechanism to influence the siting and type of tourism development by confining development to specified areas where environmental impact would be minimised.

— Adopt planning measures to reduce emissions of CO_2 and other greenhouse gases, reduce pollution and the generation of wastes, and promote sound waste management.

— Introduce new or amended planning or related legislation where necessary.

Legislation & Standards

a. Legislative Framework

b. Environmental Standards

c. Regional Standards

Legislative Framework: Support implementation of sustainable tourism through an effective legislative framework that establishes standards for land use in tourism development, tourism facilities, management and investment in tourism.

— Strengthen institutional frameworks for enforcement of legislation to improve their effectiveness where necessary.

— Standardise legislation and simplify regulations and regulatory structures to improve clarity and remove inconsistencies.

— Strengthen regulations for coastal zone management and the creation of protected areas, both marine and land-based, and their enforcement, as appropriate.

— Provide a flexible legal framework for tourism destinations to develop their own set of rules and regulations applicable within their boundaries to suit the specific circumstances of their local economic, social and environmental situations, while maintaining consistency with overall national and regional objectives and minimum standards.

— Promote a better understanding between stakeholders of their differentiated roles and their shared responsibility to make tourism sustainable.

Environmental Standards: Protect the environment by setting clear ambient environmental quality standards, along with targets for reducing pollution from all sectors, including tourism, to achieve these standards, and by preventing development in areas where it would be inappropriate.

— Minimise pollution at source, for example, by waste minimisation, recycling, and appropriate effluent treatment.

— Take into account the need to reduce emissions of CO_2 and other greenhouse gases resulting from travel and the tourism industry.

Regional Standards: Ensure that tourism and the environment are mutually supportive at a regional level through cooperation and coordination between States, to establish common approaches to incentives, environmental policies, and integrated tourism development planning.

— Adopt overall regional frameworks within which States may wish to jointly set their own targets, incentive and environmental policies, standards and regulations, to maximise benefits from tourism and avoid environmental deterioration from tourism activities.

— Consider regional collaboration for integrated tourism development planning.

— Develop mechanisms for measuring progress, such as indicators for sustainable tourism.

— Develop regional strategies to address transboundary environmental issues, such as marine pollution from shipping and from land-based sources of pollution.

Management of Tourism

a. Initiatives by Industry

b. Monitoring

c. Technology

d. compliance mechanism

Initiatives by Industry: Ensure long-term commitments and improvements to develop and promote sustainable tourism, through partnerships and voluntary initiatives by all sectors and stakeholders, including initiatives to give local communities a share in the ownership and benefits of tourism.

— Structure initiatives to give all stakeholders a share in the ownership, to maximise their effectiveness.

— Establish clear responsibilities, boundaries and timetables for the success of any initiative.

— As well as global initiatives, encourage small and medium-sized enterprises to also develop and promote their own initiatives for sustainable tourism at a more local level

— Consider integrating initiatives for small and medium-sized enterprises within overall business support packages, including access to financing, training and marketing, alongside measures to improve sustainability as well as the quality and diversity of their tourism products.

— Market tourism in a manner consistent with sustainable development of tourism.

Monitoring: Ensure consistent monitoring and review of tourism activities to detect problems at an early stage and to enable action to prevent the possibility of more serious damage.

— Establish indicators for measuring the overall progress of tourist areas towards sustainable development.

— Establish institutional and staff capacity for monitoring.

— Monitor the implementation of environmental protection and related measures set out in EIAs, and their effectiveness, taking into account the effectiveness of any ongoing management requirements for the effective operation and maintenance of those measures for protection of areas where tourism activities take place.

Technology: Minimise resource use and the generation of pollution and wastes by using and promoting environmentally-sound technologies (ESTs) for tourism and associated infrastructure.

— Develop and implement international agreements which include provisions to assist in the transfer of Environmentally Sound Technologies (ESTs) for the tourism sector, such as the Clean Development Mechanism of the Kyoto Protocol for energy-related issues.

— Promote introduction and more widespread use of ESTs by tourism enterprises and public authorities dealing with tourism or related infrastructures, as appropriate, including the use of renewable energy and ESTs for sanitation, water supply, and minimisation of the production of wastes generated by tourism facilities and those brought to port by cruise ships.

Compliance Mechanisms: Ensure compliance with development plans, planning conditions, standards and targets for sustainable tourism by providing incentives, monitoring compliance, and enforcement activities where necessary.

— Provide sufficient resources for maintaining compliance, including increasing the number of trained staff able to undertake enforcement activities as part of their duties.

— Monitor environmental conditions and compliance with legislation, regulations, and consent conditions

— Use compliance mechanisms and structured monitoring to help detect problems at an early stage, enabling action to be taken to prevent the possibility of more serious damage.

— Take into account compliance and reporting requirements set out in relevant international agreements.

— Use incentives to encourage good practice, where appropriate.

Conditions for Success

a. Involvement of stakeholders

b. Information Exchange

c. Capacity Building

Involvement of Stakeholders: Increase the long-term success of tourism projects by involving all primary stakeholders, including the local community, the tourism industry, and the government, in the development and implementation of tourism plans.

— Involve all primary stakeholders in the development and implementation of tourism plans, in order to enhance their success. (Projects are most successful where all main stakeholders are involved.)

— Encourage development of partnerships with primary stakeholders to give them ownership shares in projects and a shared responsibility for success.

Information Exchange: Raise awareness of sustainable tourism and its implementation by promoting exchange of information between governments and all stakeholders, on best practice for sustainable tourism, and establishment of networks for dialogue on implementation of these Principles; and promote broad understanding are awareness to strengthen attitudes, values and actions that are compatible with sustainable development.

— Exchange information between governments and all stakeholders, on best practice for sustainable tourism development and management, including information on planning, standards, legislation and enforcement, and of experience gained in implementation of these Principles.

— Use International and regional organisations, including UNEP, can assist with information exchange.

— Encourage development of networks for the exchange of views and information.

Capacity Building: Ensure effective implementation of sustainable tourism, and these Principles, through capacity building programmes to develop and strengthen human resources and institutional capacities in government at national and local levels, and amongst local communities; and to integrate environmental and human ecological considerations at all levels.

— Develop and strengthen their human resources and institutional capacities to facilitate the effective implementation of these Principles.

— Transfer know-how and provide training in areas related to sustainability in tourism, such as planning, legal framework, standards setting, administration and regulatory control, and the application of impact assessment and management techniques and procedures to tourism.

— Facilitate the transfer and assimilation of new environmentally-sound, socially acceptable and appropriate technology and know-how.

— Encourage contributions to capacity-building from the local, national, regional and international levels by countries, international organisations, the private sector and tourism industry, and NGOs.

— Encourage assistance from those involved in tourism in countries which have not yet been able to implement sustainability mechanisms in training at the local and national level in the sustainable development of tourism in co-operation with the Governments concerned.

CHAPTER 8

TOUR OPERATION: OPPORTUNITIES AND CHALLENGES

The tourism industry is one of the largest industry in the world. It depends on a wide range of infrastructure services — airports, air navigation, roads, railheads and ports, as well as basic infrastructure services required by hotels, restaurants, shops, and recreation facilities. It is the combination of tourism and good infrastructure that underpins the economic, environmental and social benefits. It is important to balance any decision to develop an area for tourism against the need to preserve fragile or threatened environments and cultures. However, once a decision has been taken where an area is appropriate for new tourism development, or that an existing tourist site should be developed further, then good infrastructure will be essential to sustain the quality, economic viability and growth of tourism industry. Good infrastructure will also be a key factor in the industry's ability to manage visitor flows in ways that do not affect the natural or built heritage, nor counteract against local interests.

For the last three decades tourism industry growth has been a major contributor to increased economic activity throughout the the world. It has created jobs in both large and small communities and is a major industry in many places. It is the dominant economic activity in some communities. Yet, the impacts of tourism to a community are not widely understood—even where tourism is growing dramatically and should be of the greatest interest or concern. Most people think of tourism in terms of economic impacts, jobs, and taxes. However, the range of impacts from tourism is broad and often influences areas beyond those commonly associated with tourism. Leaders as well as residents who understand the potential impacts of tourism can integrate this industry into their community in the most positive way.

POTENTIAL IMPACTS OF TOURISM

Specific plans and actions can increase tourism's benefits or decrease the gravity of a negative impact. It is important for communities to understand the wide scope of impacts and endeavor to agree on what positive impacts to emphasize. It is wise to acknowledge and identify possible negative impacts so actions can be taken to minimize or prevent them. A clear statement of the community's vision of tourism should be an integral part of a community's comprehensive plan. Active planning directs tourism toward the goals of the community, clarifying tourism's role and uniting multiple interests.

Planning is not enough. Active implementation and management of plans and prompt attention to emerging tourism issues will maximize positive and minimize negative impacts. Monitoring and addressing community attitudes should be an ongoing part of the management effort. Good monitoring efforts can identify trouble areas and give leaders an opportunity to defuse community reactions and make timely changes before a crisis occurs. Unfortunately, few communities are so proactive.

A goal of developing the tourism industry in a community is maximizing selected positive impacts while minimizing potential negative impacts. First, it is essential to identify the possible impacts. Tourism researchers have identified a large number of impacts. Grouping the impacts into categories shows the types of impacts that could result from developing tourism in a community. The following tables list a range of important tourism impacts in a concise format. Readers needing additional information about specific impacts should contact appropriate professionals or consult tourism texts and research papers.

A community will not experience every impact. Some are dependent on particular natural resource features (mountains, coral reefs) or development and spatial patterns (special "tourist zones"). Others relate to the social condition of the community, particularly the ability to culturally or socially connect with tourists. Still others relate to types and intensity of tourism developments, i.e., approval or hostility toward tourist activities. The following tables are extensive but not all-inclusive.

Understanding that tourism development may result in many and complex impacts suggests that local elected officials, the tourism industry, and community residents need to work cooperatively and carefully to plan for its growth and development. Planning can help create an industry that enhances a community with minimal costs and disruptions in other aspects of community life. Having broad community involvement and embracing different perspectives during planning helps identify and resolve concerns that would otherwise create problems later.

Economic Impacts

Tourism increases employment opportunities. Additional jobs, ranging from low-wage entry-level to high-paying professional positions in management and technical fields, in public utilities such as water, sewer, sidewalks, lighting, parking, public restrooms, litter control, and landscaping. Such improvements benefit tourists and residents alike. Likewise, tourism encourages improvements in transport infrastructure resulting in upgraded roads, airports, public transportation, and non-traditional transportation (e.g., trails). Tourism encourages new elements to join the retail mix, increasing opportunities for shopping and adding healthy competitiveness. It often increases a community's tax revenues. Lodging and sales taxes most notably increase but additional tax revenues include air travel and other transportation taxes, business taxes, and fuel taxes. New jobs generate more income tax revenues.

When considering the economic impacts of tourism, it is essential to understand that tourism businesses often include a significant number of low-paying jobs, often at minimum wage or less. These jobs are often seasonal, causing under-employment or unemployment during off-seasons. Labor may be imported, rather than hired locally, especially if particular skills or expertise is required, or if local labor is unavailable. Some tourism-related businesses are volatile and high-risk ventures that are unsustainable. Greater demand for goods, services, land, and housing may increase prices that in turn will increase the cost of living.

Tourism businesses may claim land that could have higher- value or other uses. Additionally, non-local owners and corporations may export profits out of the community. The community may have to generate funds (possibly through increased taxes) to maintain roads and transportation systems that have become more heavily used. Similarly, if additional infrastructure is required, additional taxes may also be needed to pay for them.

Environmental Impacts

Areas with high-value natural resources, like oceans, lakes, waterfalls, mountains, unique flora and fauna, and great scenic beauty attract tourists and new residents (in-migrants) who seek emotional and spiritual connections with nature. Because these people value nature, selected natural environments are preserved, protected, and kept from further ecological decline. Lands that could be developed can generate income by accommodating the recreational activities of visitors. Tourist income often makes it possible to preserve and restore historic buildings and monuments. Improvements in the area's appearance through cleanup or repairs and the addition of public art such as murals, water fountains, and monuments (part of making a community ready for tourism) benefit visitors and residents alike. Tourism is generally considered a "clean" industry, one that is based on hotels, restaurants, shops and attractions, instead of factories.

Tourism can also degrade an environment. Visitors generate waste and pollution (air, water, solid waste, noise, and visual). Natural resource attractions can be jeopardized through improper uses or overuse. Providing tourist services can alter the landscape's appearance. For instance, visual pollution may occur from billboard proliferation. As tourism develops, demand for land increases, especially for prime locations like beachfronts, special views, and mountains.

Without forethought, natural landscape and open space can be lost. The destruction or loss of flora and fauna can happen when desirable plants and animals are collected for sale or the land is trampled. Tourists or the businesses that cater to them often remove plants, animals, rocks, fossils, coral, and cultural or historical artifacts from an area. Uncontrolled visitation or overuse by visitors can degrade landscapes, historic sites, and monuments. Where water is scarce, tourists can overwhelm the available supply. Travelers can also inadvertently introduce nonindigenous species, as can increases in the trade of animals and plants. A constant stream of visitors and domestic pets may disrupt wildlife by disturbing their breeding cycles and altering natural behaviors.

Social and Cultural Impacts

The social and cultural ramifications of tourism warrant careful consideration, as impacts can either become assets or detriments to communities. Influxes of tourists bring diverse values to the community and influence behaviors and family life. Individuals and the collective community might try to please tourists or adopt tourist behaviors. Interactions between residents, and tourists can impact creative expression by providing new opportunities (positive) or by stifling individuality with new restrictions (negative). Increased tourism can push a community to adopt a different moral conduct such as improved understanding between sexes (positive) or increased illicit drug use (negative).

Safety and health facilities and staffing tend to increase at the same time safety problems such as crime and accidents increase. Traditonal ceremonies may be renewed and revived by tourist interest or lost in alternative activities. Community organizations can be invigorated by facing the opportunities of tourism or overwhelmed by its associated problems. Calamities such as natural disasters, energy shortages, terrorism, political upheaval, disease outbreak, a chemical spill, or even widespread negative publicity could shut down tourism abruptly but sometimes can attract curious visitors.

Tourism can improve the quality of life in an area by increasing the number of attractions, recreational opportunities, and services. Tourism offers residents opportunities to meet interesting people, make friendships, learn about the world, and expose themselves to new perspectives. Experiencing different cultural practices enriches experiences, broadens horizons, and increases insight and appreciation for different approaches to living. Often, dwindling interest in host cultures is revived by reawakening cultural heritage as part of tourism development, which increases demand for historical and cultural exhibits. This interest by tourists in local culture and history provides opportunities to support preservation of historical artifacts and architecture. By learning more about others, their differences become less threatening and more interesting. At the same time, tourism often promotes higher levels of psychological satisfaction from opportunities created by tourism development and through interactions with travelers.

Tourism can come to a community with a dark social and cultural side, too. Illegal activities tend to increase in the relaxed atmosphere of tourist areas. Increased underage drinking can become a problem especially in beach communities, areas with festivals involving alcohol, and ski villages. It is easier to be anonymous where strangers are taken for granted; bustling tourist traffic can increase the presence of smugglers and buyers of smuggled products. Lifestyle changes such as alterations in local travel patterns to avoid tourist congestion and the avoidance of downtown shopping can damage a community socially and culturally. Hotels, restaurants, and shops can push tourism development into residential areas, forcing changes in the physical structure of a community.

Development of tourist facilities in prime locations may cause locals to be or feel excluded from those resources. As local ethnic culture alters to fit the needs of tourism, language and cultural practices may change. In places where longer- term visitors tend to congregate, social cliques, such as condo tourists or RVers, may be at odds with local interests and work to influence local issues. The "demonstration effect" of tourists (residents adopting tourist behaviors) and the addition of tourist facilities may alter customs, such as dating habits, especially those of a more structured or traditional culture. The potential of meeting and marrying non-local mates may create family stress.Community Attitude

Visitor interest and satisfaction in the community is a source of local pride. Seeing visitor interest makes local residents more appreciative of local resources that are often taken for granted. As tourism develops, local residents will enjoy more facilities and a greater range of choices. Tourism activities and events tend to make living in a place more interesting and exciting. However, heightened tension and community divisiveness can occur over tourism development, pitting tourism supporters against non-supporters.

Tension between residents and tourists can occur. People will often feel stressed over the new, increasingly hectic community and personal pace of life. They may claim the result is no better than before or perhaps even worse. Where culture is part of the tourist attractions, over-amplification of cultural traits and creation of "new" cultural traits to satisfy tourist tastes may create a phony culture. Residents may experience a sense of exclusion and alienation over planning and development concerns.

They may feel a loss of control over the community's future as "outsiders" take over establishments and new development. Over-dependence on non-local developers and an influx of outside businesses creates a sense that the community is being manipulated and exploited by outsiders for the sole benefit of those developers or business people. Hotels built in monolithic cubes or restaurants with standardized franchise designs might clash with local standards and disrupt the aesthetic appearance of the community, damage unique community character, and spread "sameness."

People congregate in attractive places. Tourism often develops around specific locations and concentrates there, providing growth yet avoiding sprawl. Historic buildings and grounds, which might otherwise slowly deteriorate, have great appeal for tourism development and can often be renovated to suit the industry.

As people congregate, congestion and crowding produces stress, annoyance, anger, and other negative attitudes. Hordes of visitors may impede local businesses, prevent residents from accomplishing normal activities, and compete for space. Tourism construction, especially hotels, may be inappropriate in scale and style with respect to other structures and the landscape. In some areas, recreational second homes and condominium developments create major crowding and congestion problems.

Service Opportunities

Tourism creates opportunities to develop new amenities and recreation facilities that would not otherwise be viable in a community. Tourist expectations can upgrade service by local shops, restaurants, and other commerce operators. Tourist traffic in a community creates an opportunity for upgraded fire, police, and medical protection that also benefits residents.

Traditional services may be forced out or relocated due to competition with tourist interests. Supply shortages may occur, temporarily, seasonally, or chronically. Water, power, fuel, and other shortages may be experienced with increased pressure on the infrastructure.

Tax Revenue

Increased retail activity from restaurants and tourist shopping will add state and local sales tax revenue. Lodging tax revenue to the city (or state) should increase since travelers account for virtually all lodging tax receipts. Increased tax burdens to expand infrastructure and public services will be passed on to property owners through increased property taxes.

CHALLENGES OF TOUR OPERATORS

Tour operators obtain information, make contracts with suppliers of services, and publish their holiday offers in brochures, which are distributed directly to consumers or by travel agents. Tour operators judge overall demand and the expected demand for each destination and seek to satisfy that demand if it can be accomplished profitably. Present in substantial numbers in Europe and in the United States, Canada, Japan, South Korea, Russia, Australia, New Zealand, South and Latin America, tour operators remain small in number where tourism is less developed. Globally, they represent around 12% of international arrivals, while in Europe they account for 35% of leisure air holidays. There are five substantial European outbound tour operators, the remaining 4, 995 being SMEs employing five to 100 people, which often cater for specialist interests or low volume destinations. The five large companies have integrated activities (travel agencies, tour operations, airlines, hotels, cruise ships and ground handling), but these are not exclusively used by the one integrated organisation.

Economic Challenges

Tour operating employs relatively few people across the world (a few tens of thousands) , but their activities can stimulate hotel and infrastructure development. These include water, sewerage, airports, roads etc, transport services, agriculture, information technology, restaurants, entertainment and media, education and training, consumption of pharmaceutical products, clothing, equipment, medical services, excursion venues and public administration concerned with policy-making, marketing and management of tourism. While tour operators have a limited number of staff in some of their receiving countries, a huge network of activities and jobs across the economy depend upon delivering the demand for tourism. The marketing efforts of tour operators are what the suppliers of services and governments look for.

Tour operators can have a significant impact upon economies. Whereas the Balearic Islands were the poorest province in the whole of Spain in 1950, by the year 2000 it was the richest – almost entirely due to organised tourism. The Maldives is no longer to be classified as a 'lesser developed country' thanks to the economic impact of tourism, operator industry particularly organised tourism. Cancun in Mexico had a local population of 600 before tourism arrived. It now provides income for 600, 000 and support for ten times that number through organised tourism from North and South America, and Europe. In Turkey, tourism revenues reach 30% of total commodity exports, most attributed to organised tourism.

Foreign exchange received by countries through tour operators takes the form of payments to hotels and ground handlers as well as taxes, duties and charges. In addition, consumers spend money outside the hotel on the 'complementary offer'. This amount can vary from 150% of the hotel cost in countries such Spain to virtually zero in those developing countries that offer little to see, do or buy.

Outbound tourism demand is affected by confidence in economic conditions and security as well as perceptions of discretionary income. Leisure outbound travel has been growing at around one and a half times the growth in GDP and is not highly volatile, unless there are safety concerns. Fluctuations tourism revenues in receiving countries are more marked due to consumer perceptions of the relative safety and attractiveness of destinations, as well as changes in relative price.

Socio-cultutal Challenges

The ability to travel and to witness other cultures not only brings prosperity to the receiving country, but also fosters understanding and tolerance in the visitor. The tour operator offer – based on high volumes, bulk buying and low prices – has provided access to travel to millions of people. Tour operator's main contribution has been to increase tourism volume in many destinations that would otherwise have had little tourism development. However, the way in which different countries and destinations have dealt with the effects of this increase varies widely. By far the most positive influence of tourism has been on the citizens of the receiver countries, where the foreign influx has provided income for much greater social choices than have hitherto existed and accelerated the process of modernisation and openness.

As local people have become richer through tourism, countries dependent on international tourism have found themselves generating a greater number of domestic tourists. The effect of this phenomenon in Spain, for example, has been the restoration of a strong Spanish identity – both cultural and culinary – which had been weakened. Tour operator distribution has created jobs in originating countries, particularly for women in travel agencies, airlines, airports and hotels as well as for tour operators themselves.

Negative social consequences have been felt in a number of different and significant ways. The 'homogenisation' of global products and services devoid of local identity has been exacerbated by tourism movements. There is no doubt that people brought for a short time to another country seek to retain their own habits and practices – while host communities adapt to satisfy visitor tastes in order to make money from them. Those with vulnerable cultures are likely to suffer most and local disaffection is most keenly felt where there are high densities of tourists. Reaction tends to come from regional, religious or cultural entities attempting to preserve key features that provide a manifestation of a local identity.

Overall, the opportunity for jobs in tourism and tourism-related activities in receiving countries have been very positive, as has the opportunity for training and development. However, a major market failure has been the inability to develop and diversify the complementary offer (things to see, buy or do outside the hotel) that would provide extra jobs and income in the community and allow monies to be distributed more widely and deeply This remains a significant opportunity to alleviate poverty in some developing countries. In countries where the money economy is limited and unemployment high, tourism can be seen to benefit the few who are directly involved in tourism, leaving workers in the informal economy marginalised and disaffected. In addition, children vulnerable to sexual exploitation have found themselves targeted by a small number of paedophiles.

Tour operators have many sub-contracted suppliers that are expected to deliver quality services under some form of supervision. They rely upon close relationships with people working in the destinations – at airports, hotels, restaurants, excursion venues, public administrations, medical authorities, etc. – for without them, holidays could not be delivered. Tour operators have resident staff, or those of their local agents that maintain these relationships and are expected to become familiar with concerns expressed by local communities.

Where good quality accommodation for customers is in short supply, many tour operators co-finance developments on a short-term basis. Tour operators act as a bridge between suppliers, customers and the country visited, providing information about the destination, safety and cultural sensitivity (dress codes, etc). With smaller guided tours, customers often seek greater detailed interaction and are very aware of their social and cultural responsibilities.

The International Federation of Tour Operators (IFTO) acts as the spokesperson for tour operators (and their clients) with municipalities, regional and national governments and international organisations such as the WTO/OMT, UNCTAD, WHO, UNESCO, UNEP, and the EU. Issues range from the broadest level to the narrowest dealings with the public administration involve ministries of foreign affairs, home affairs, public works, environment, transport, tourism, education, health and finance. the private sector, all the actors in tourism and related to tourism are involved in discussions. As tourism is a horizontal activity, co-ordination, consultation and partnerships are essential for it be successful.

Environmental Challenges

The direct environmental impact of tour operators is relatively limited, but there are ways in which they can have a positive influence. Tour operators communicate with customers mainly through paper-based media, therefore brochures need to be used efficiently and to be sourced from renewable forests and recycled whenever possible. Offices need to consume as little energy as possible and customers need to be encouraged to make choices and to behave in ways that are socially and environmentally acceptable. considering the indirect effects of tour operators encouraging people to travel, a distinction needs to be made between developed and developing nations when considering environmental action. Developed nations have the technical and financial resources to monitor and enforce environmental standards in tourism development and, in many cases, the political to act as well as a body of planning regulations. In these circumstances, should a problem arise a basis for negotiation exists between the governing authorities and the local tourism actors together with IFTO.

Developing countries may have priorities that are more pressing than sustainable development in tourism. There may be neither the political will nor the technical or financial resources to monitor environmental performance. In these situations it is important for the tour operator and other tourism actors to adopt self-regulation. For example, in the Antarctic where no legal framework exists and the environment is highly vulnerable, tour operators and cruise ships have signed up to a defined code of conduct. This is weaker than a legal solution as no effective sanctions can be applied to those not adhering to the code.

Tour operators encourage people to travel from their local airport, which usually means a taxi or a car journey. (A taxi journey is twice as long as that by the owner-driver, and doubles energy consumption/emissions). Airports have been extended as a result of consumer demand – larger aircraft are now used. Tour operators seek out the lowest seat mile costs – this requires in turn, high-density seating and fuel-efficient modern aircraft operating at high load factors.

The resulting emissions of noise, CO_2 and NO_x per passenger are lower than for other forms of aviation, but nonetheless would not have occurred had customers stayed at home. Customers are usually transported from the destination airport to the hotel by modern diesel-engined or gas-powered coaches which can carry up to 58 people and have low seat/mile CO_2 emissions. These vehicles reduce the incidence of car traffic by more than 25 times. However, in many developing countries these are not available; LPG (liquid petroleum gas) or CNG (compressed nitrogen gas) distribution is extremely limited.

While at the hotel, visitor energy consumption/ emissions due to air-conditioning is broadly equivalent to energy consumption/emissions through central heating at home unless, as in Cyprus, all tourist establishments are required to install solar panels, in which case energy consumption by tourists will be less than that by residents. In beach destinations where movement outside hotels is limited to excursions, consumption/emissions during a two-week stay are likely to be much less than staying at home.

The huge majority of tourists fly from colder to warmer climates in countries with beaches nearer the equator, which get less rain and have less available water. Although tourism uses very little water compared with agriculture, there is a significant increase in the consumption of water as a result of tourism. De-salination plants have been installed in some areas of high-density tourism where there are water shortages. Hotels pay for water consumption by volume and this is reflected in prices to consumers. Many hotels employ systems to reduce consumption of water and energy consumption and waste, but this remains a major issue in much of the developed and developing world.

Sewerage systems are expensive and 'high tech' systems are required to avoid contamination of seawater. These may be funded through central/local government and through multi-lateral sources. Huge investments have taken place in coastal areas of high tourism density, but much remains to be done. Likewise, solid waste is a major issue for many municipalities operating in tourism areas.

Where construction of airports, roads, hotels and other infrastructure is concerned, planning regulations that determine maximum spread and density are required to maintain an appropriate balance. Where local governance is weak there are frequent examples of over development. The degradation of heritage sites that suffer from visitor congestion is another issue, which has yet to be dealt with satisfactorily.

In the past ten years, a lot of progress has been made. Firstly, information to consumers by tour operators has vastly improved although there are still no objective international measures to indicate to consumers the environmental performance of sub-contracted suppliers or destinations. A plethora of eco-labels exist, but none with global credibility. Secondly, tour operators have developed and attempt to comply with codes of conduct, with some success.

The response of tour operators to global warming issues relating to emissions has been to encourage zero emission engine manufacture and ensure that emissions per passenger are the lowest currently available economically by using modern fuel-efficient aircraft and coaches with high-density seating.

In terms of indirect impact, where tour operators have been accepted as legitimate partners in tourism development in many countries and destinations, there is the opportunity for the tour operator to be influenced by, as well as to influence, the behaviour of various public and private sector actors in the destinations. However, results are very varied both between and within countries.

It is in the area of tourism management that the large tour operators have sought to influence the public and private sectors. Many tour operators seek to monitor the environmental performance of sub-contracted suppliers and destinations. They support countries and regions in implementing the development processes of local 'Agenda 21s' and actively promote the harmonisation of local, communal and regional needs in tourism development plans. They support measures that help in visitor management and make their own staff aware of sustainable development needs. Strong governance and institutional frameworks have helped to manage flows of tourism through tour operators in most developed nations, although more could be accomplished.

In the developing world this has been less effective with the exception of low volume specialist destinations, which have benefited from responsible management policies of tour operators. It is in the few developing countries with volumes of tourists that are not appropriate for the habitat or current infrastructure that problems can arise. It should be emphasised that multi-stakeholder involvement in receiving countries/ destinations can only be effective if tour operators are included as active partners.

In the end it is for the country/destination to determine what role tourism should play in their community and what policies they want to follow. Attempts by outsiders (e. g. tour operators or NGOs) to create solutions based on 'western criteria' are almost certain to fail.

Key areas for improvement include:

— tour operators need to develop a responsible tourism policy;

— better information to consumers from tour operators, particularly on credible environmental standards applied to and monitored among sub-contracted suppliers;

— stronger relationships with tour operators and local public-private sector actors in all significant tourism destinations to support destination management policies aimed at sustainable development. This should lead to constructive consultation as well as the emergence of true local partnerships;

— significant development of the 'complementary offer' to create jobs among women and the local community in developing countries, and greater development of local agriculture to provide specific foods for tourists;

— encouragement of zero-emission terrestrial vehicles and aircraft;

— management of water, waste and energy consumption and the protection of tourism sites (heritage and natural) from unmanaged tourism flows that degrade both the natural environment and the visitor experience;

— encourage tour operators to adopt self-regulation through appropriate codes of conduct specific to habitat and destination where there are insufficient governance and institutional frameworks;

— raising tour operators' awareness of the social dimension of sustainable development and ensuring that policies and communications to consumers reflect local community concerns;

— tour operators need to ensure those sustainable tourism development concepts, procedures and practices are included in their management and representative training programmes;

— tour operators need to set goals for sustainable development against which their performance can be measured and reported both internally and publicly.

Tour operators use a variety of tools to create feedback systems to alert the tour operators as well as public and private actors in the destinations.

— TUI, a part of Preussag, one of the largest tour operators in the world, with 23 million customers, and Scandinavian Leisure Group, part of MyTravel, track the environmental performance of destinations and sub-contracted suppliers;

— Many of the small tour operators have clear guidelines for their staff to follow and report back on adverse consequences of their tourism activity. Customers, too, are quick to bring to the attention of tour operators' adverse consequences. NGOs can also contribute their views; the issues raised are commonly dealt with through the local contacts of tour operators in the destination. Otherwise, in a destination with high volumes of tourists, IFTO is often used to communicate the adverse consequences and recommend remedial action; more recently, the Tour Operator Initiative has provided the beginnings of a network of tour operators large and small, to develop better policies and systems of implementation;

— IFTO has played an active and prominent role with WTO/OMT by chairing its Business Council. Sustainable development is a key part of WTO/OMT's programme of work.

Challnges of Incoming Tour Operator

Most international visitors are unfamiliar with the countries they visit. To assist them plan operate their itineraries, hotels, visits and attractions, the role of the incoming tour operator, agent or groundhandler has emerged. Many are simply organised as a service to customers, others have broadened the scope of their activities through backward integration by buying coach companies and hotels. With the emergence of outbound tour operators, the role of the incoming tour operator has been much enhanced. Contracts are made between the two to deliver transfers and excursions and (on occasions) hotels.

The incoming tour operator provides all logistical support as well as providing local knowledge (commercial, legal, political and environmental) on what can and cannot be done. Very few incoming tour operators have been acquired by outbound tour operators, and 99% remain as local independent businesses. Worldwide there are many thousands of incoming tour operators.

In developing countries, in particular, these local businesses compete to represent tour operators and those that fail resent that all the business of the outbound tour operator goes through one local business. The incoming tour operator attempts to create a range of offers to attract consumers that are practical in terms of logistics and the environment and provide the right price/value to consumers and profits to themselves. From the perspective of the suppliers in the receiving destination, the incoming tour operator forms part of their destination network for which they are prepared to pay.

The outbound tour operator can also play a role in that distribution to customers. The coach companies play a crucial role in the batch distribution of customers from airport to hotels and on tours to excursion venues. Their fleets are, in the main, very modern and well maintained. The rent-a-car companies usually provide new or nearly new vehicles for hire. The economic value of rent-a-cars for tourism is that customers can reach destinations not accessible without motorised transport.

The major attractions act as magnets to tourists providing the motivation for visits and leading to increased use of hotel rooms, roads, airports, rail transport as well as the land use for the attraction itself. They can provide a major drive for increased local employment. Major attractions depend on very high visitor throughput.

The incoming tour operators can, and do, lay down clear policies and procedures for subcontracted suppliers to follow to protect the environment and to support enlightened social policies. However, these local businesses are run on local labour law, regulations, custom and practice.

In some developing countries, the custom and practice may not meet the standards demanded, for example, by International Labour Organization (ILO) . Outbound tour operators can have influence over how their passengers are handled by the incoming tour operators/suppliers, however, they have no influence on how the incoming tour operator arranges for the majority of their work with their suppliers that takes place with individuals on independently organised groups.

The incoming tour operators recognise that they have a significant role to play in tourism development. Their decisions on excursion venues and planning of trips can have strong impacts on particular communities. These communities are in competition with each other for offering attractions to tourists who have limited time. Tourists will often go to one craft market, but not two, so decisions by incoming tour operators count heavily.

The obligation of the coach companies is to ensure that the vehicles are safe and secure and emit the lowest emissions possible with the use of local fuels. Their social obligations relate to conditions of work, particularly drivers' hours, as well as driving and parking procedures.

The opportunities for incoming tour operators are to be recognised for the important and influential role they can play in tourism development. As small local enterprises, they are often not brought into policy discussions with government at the appropriate level. The challenges for incoming tour operators, agents and groundhandlers are:

— to obtain from government recognition of their influential role,

— to take a balanced and responsible approach to the provision of services that they provide within the context and possibilities of their local conditions,

— to influence their subcontracted suppliers to adopt a similar balanced responsible approach.

Concerns for the Future

Tour operators should set the goal of introducing a comprehensive responsible tourism policy covering direct action and indirect impacts, within the next five years.

Tour operators direct action:

— better information to consumers;

— more use of electronic communication;

— reduction in use of paper;

— better use of recycled paper and paper from renewable forests;

— eliminate use of toxic paper coating;

— aggregate performance data to support corporate annual reporting and year on year improvements,

— ensure that sustainable development concepts, procedures and practices are included in management and training programmes;

— ensure greater adherence to tour operator codes of conduct.

Success in the above areas will depend on:

— the development of agreed international criteria against which to measure the environmental performance of subcontracted suppliers in order to keep consumers better informed;

— the extent of the use of electronic means of communication;

— technological innovation and progress that will allow the development of low cost, thin (low weight) shiny paper for brochures that have high levels of environmental performance.

Tour operators indirect impacts:

— tour operators need to improve their monitoring of the social and environmental performance of sub-contracted suppliers and destinations;

— tour operators should develop stronger relationships with local public and private sector actors in all significant tourism destinations, to support destination management policies and strategies aimed at sustainable development.

In addition, tour operators need to:

— protect the natural environment and cultural heritage,

— conserve plants and animals, protected areas and landscapes,

— respect the integrity of local cultures and their social institutions.

BIBLIOGRAPHY

Chambers, Erve (ed.). *Tourism and Culture: An Applied Perspective.* Albany: State University Press of New York, 1997.

Drummond, Siobhan and Ian Yeoman (eds.). *Quality Issues in Heritage Visitor Attractions.* Oxford: Butterworth / Heinemann, 2001.

Foehr, Stephen, *Eco-Journeys: The World Guide to Ecologically Aware Travel and Adventure,* Chicago, IL: Noble Press, 1993. Biodiv G155 .A1 F63 1993.

Godde, P, Price, M, F M Zimmermann, *Tourism and Development in Mountain Regions,* 2000

Goodwin, Harold. *Tourism, Conservation, and Sustainable Development: Case Studies from Asia and Africa.* London: International Institute for Environment and Development, 1998. Biodiv HD8039 .T642 I44 1998.

Grubbs, Bruce. *Desert Hiking Tips: Expert Advice on Desert Hiking and Driving.* Helena, MT: Falcon, c1998. Pub GV200.5 .G78 1998.

Harris, Rob, Tony Griffin and Peter Williams. *Sustainable Tourism: A Global Perspective.* Oxford: Butterworth-Heinemann, 2002.

Honey, Martha. *Ecotourism and Sustainable Development: Who Owns Paradise?* Washington, D.C.: Island Press, 1999.

Horner, Susan, John Swarbrooke, *International Cases in Tourism Management,* 2004

John Tribe, *The Economics of Leisure and Tourism,* Business & Economics, 1999

Joseph Sirgy M., *New Dimensions in Marketing/Quality-Of-Life Research* 1995

Judd, Dennis R. and Susan S. Fainstein (eds.). *The Tourist City*. New Haven: Yale University Press, 1999.

Kerr W., *Tourism Public Policy, and the Strategic Management of Failure*, 2003

Kirchenblatt-Gimblett, Barbara. *Destination Culture: Tourism, Museums, and Heritage*. Berkeley: University of California Press, 1998.

Mann Mark, *The Community Tourism Guide*, 2000

INDEX